POLAND IN THE TWENTIETH CENTURY

Also by Peter D. Stachura

NAZI YOUTH IN THE WEIMAR REPUBLIC

THE WEIMAR ERA AND HITLER: A Select Bibliography

THE SHAPING OF THE NAZI STATE (*editor*)

* THE GERMAN YOUTH MOVEMENT, 1900–1945: An Interpretative and Documentary History

THE NAZI MACHTERGREIFUNG (*editor*)

GREGOR STRASSER AND THE RISE OF NAZISM

* UNEMPLOYMENT AND THE GREAT DEPRESSION IN WEIMAR GERMANY (*editor*)

* THE WEIMAR REPUBLIC AND THE YOUNGER PROLETARIAT: An Economic and Social Analysis

POLITICAL LEADERS IN WEIMAR GERMANY

THEMES OF MODERN POLISH HISTORY (*editor*)

* POLAND BETWEEN THE WARS 1918–1939 (*editor*)

* *from the same publishers*

Poland in the Twentieth Century

Peter D. Stachura
Reader in History
University of Stirling
Scotland

First published in Great Britain 1999 by
MACMILLAN PRESS LTD
Houndmills, Basingstoke, Hampshire RG21 6XS and London
Companies and representatives throughout the world

A catalogue record for this book is available from the British Library.

ISBN 0–333–75266–X

First published in the United States of America 1999 by
ST. MARTIN'S PRESS, INC.,
Scholarly and Reference Division,
175 Fifth Avenue, New York, N.Y. 10010

ISBN 0–312–22027–8

Library of Congress Cataloging-in-Publication Data
Stachura, Peter D.
Poland in the twentieth century / Peter D. Stachura.
p.   cm.
Includes bibliographical references and index.
ISBN 0–312–22027–8 (cloth)
1. Poland—History—20th century.   I. Title.   II. Title: Poland
in the 20th century.
DK4382.S73   1999
943.805—dc21   98–49490
                                                            CIP

This book is printed on paper suitable for recycling and made from fully managed and sustained forest sources.

10   9   8   7   6   5   4   3   2   1
08   07   06   05   04   03   02   01   00   99

Printed and bound in Great Britain by
Antony Rowe Ltd, Chippenham, Wiltshire

For my late Father, who experienced much of what is related herein, and my Mother

Contents

List of Abbreviations and Glossary

Agudath Israel	A conservative, pro-assimilationist Jewish political party in inter-war Poland
AK	Home Army (A*rmia Krajowa*, 1942–5)
AUEM	Amalgamated Union of Engineering Workers (British)
AWS	Solidarity Electoral Alliance (contested the Polish elections in 1997)
BBC	British Broadcasting Corporation
BBWR	*Bezpartyjny Blok dla Współpracy z Rządem* (Non-Party Bloc for Co-operation with the Government, 1928–35)
Bund	Abbreviation of the 'General Jewish Workers' Union', a Jewish Marxist and anti-Zionist political party in inter-war Poland
cheder	Jewish religious school
COP	*Centralny Okrąg Przemysłowy* (Central Industrial Area, 1936–9)
Drang nach Osten	German concept denoting the aim of expanding into Eastern Europe
Duma	Russian parliament
Endecja	Polish name for the National Democratic Party and its successors pre-1939
Endek	Polish abbreviation for member/follower of the National Democratic Party
Erfüllungspolitik	Term to describe Germany's compliance with the Treaty of Versailles in the mid-1920s under Foreign Minister Gustav Stresemann

Folkists

Small Jewish political party in inter-war Poland

Gestapo

Geheimes Staatspolizei (Nazi Secret Police)

Gulag

The Soviet system of labour and detention camps, synonymous with inhumanity

HMSO

Her Majesty's Stationery Office

Holocaust

The systematic extermination of the Jews by the Nazis in the Second World War

Katyń Massacre

The murder of thousands of captured Polish officers by the Soviets in 1940

Kehile (plural *Kehillah*)

Jewish communal organizational body

KGB

Soviet Secret Police, successor to the NKVD (see below)

Knesset

Israeli parliament

KNP

Komitet Narodowy Polski (Polish National Committee, 1914–15, 1917–19)

Konarmiya

Red Cossack Cavalry of the early Bolshevik period

KPN

Konfederacja Polski Niepodległej (Confederation for an Independent Poland, a nationalist and anti-Communist party, 1976–present, led by Leszek Moczulski)

KPP

Komunistyczna Partia Polski (Communist Party of Poland, 1926–38)

Lebensraum

Germany's expansionist aims under Adolf Hitler in the East (for 'living space')

MI6

British Intelligence

NATO

North Atlantic Treaty Organization (post-1945 Western military alliance)

NKN

Naczelny Komitet Narodowy (Supreme National Committee, Kraków, 1914–17)

NKVD

Narodnaya Kommissiya Vevnutrikh Dyel (People's Commissariat for Internal Affairs – Soviet Secret Police)

Nomenklatura	Collective name for the postwar Communist power élite in Poland
NSDAP	*Nationalsozialistische Deutsche Arbeiterpartei* (Nazi Party)
NSZ	*Narodowe Siły Zbrojne* (National Armed Forces, an extreme right-wing underground military organization in Poland, 1942–4)
NUM	National Union of Mineworkers (British)
Oberleutnant	Lieutenant
ONR	*Obóz Narodowo-Radykalny* (National Radical Camp), a small extreme right-wing organization in Poland in the 1930s
Operation Barbarossa	Code-name for the German attack on the Soviet Union in 1941
Ostpolitik	The more flexible policy towards Eastern Europe pioneered by Federal German Chancellor Willy Brandt in the 1970s
OZON (or OZN)	*Obóz Zjednoczenia Narodowego* (Camp of National Unity, 1937–9)
People's Poland	The Soviet-imposed Communist regime in Poland (1944/45–1989)
PFS	*Polska Federacja Strzelecka* (Polish Riflemen's Association, pre-1914)
Polnische Wehrmacht	A small military force raised by the Germans in Poland during the First World War
PPR	*Polska Partia Robotnicza* (Polish Workers' Party, 1942–8, Communist)
PPS	*Polska Partia Socjalistyczna* (Polish Socialist Party, 1892–1948)
PRC	Polish Resettlement Corps (in Britain, 1946–9)
PSL	*Polskie Stronnictwo Ludowe* (Polish Peasant Party, 1895–1947)

PSN

Polskie Stronnictwo Narodowe (Polish National Party of the 1990s, right-wing)

PSP

Polskie Stronnictwo Postępowa (Polish Progressive Party, pre-1914, in Galicia)

PZPR

Polska Zjednoczona Partia Robotnicza (Polish United Workers' Party, created in 1948 and Communist)

RdR

Movement for the Republic (post-1989 right-wing political party in Poland)

Reichstag

Federal German parliament

Saisonstaat

Prusso-German derogatory term for Poland

Sanacja

Name given to the regime in Poland, 1926–39 (denoting a 'moral purification')

SD

Stronnictwo Demokratyczne (Democratic Party, Poland, 1938–9, left-liberal)

SDRP

Social Democratic Party of Poland (successor after 1989 to the Polish Communist Party, PZPR, see above)

Sejm

Polish parliament

Shtetl (plural *Shtetlekh*)

Small Jewish town(s) in Eastern Europe

Shechitah

Jewish ritual slaughter

SL

Stronnictwo Ludowe (united Peasant Party in Poland, 1931–49)

SLD

Democratic Alliance (left-wing political grouping in Poland in the 1990s)

Solidarność

Solidarity trade union movement in Poland, created in 1980 under Lech Wałęsa

SP

Stronnictwo Pracy (Party of Labour, an anti-*Sanacja* political party set up in 1937)

SPK

Stowarzyszenie Polskich Kombatantów (Polish Ex-Combatants' Association in UK)

SS   *Schutzstaffel* (Nazi élite formation)

TRJN   Provisional Government of National Unity (formed in Poland in 1945)

Ugoda   Short-lived Polish Government–Jewish Agreement in 1925

UK   United Kingdom

Virtuti Militari   Poland's highest military award under the Second Republic until 1945

USSR   Union of Soviet Socialist Republics (Soviet Union)

Wehrmacht   Name of the German Armed Forces during the Third Reich

YIVO   Jewish Scientific Institute for Research on Judaism, Wilno, 1925–39

Zamek   The name given to followers of a faction loyal to August Zalewski in the émigré Polish community in Britain, from the early 1950s until 1972

ZChN   Christian-National Union (Polish right-wing political party in the 1990s)

Zegota   Council for Aid to Jews (in Poland, 1942–5)

Zet   *Związek Młodzieży Polskiej* (Union of Polish Youth, founded in 1887)

Zjednoczenie   Federation – a faction in the Polish émigré community in the UK which opposed another faction, the *Zamek* (see above)

Złoty   Polish currency from 1924 (gold crown)

ŻOB   *Żydowska Organizacja Bojowa* (Jewish Combat Organisation, an underground military unit in occupied Poland)

ZORz   *Związek Odrodzenia Rzeczypospolitej* (Union for the Rebirth of the Republic, an abortive anti-*Sanacja* political movement of the mid-1930s)

ZWC   *Związek Walki Czynnej* (Union of Active Struggle, 1908–14, a Polish paramilitary unit)

Żydokomuna   Polish opprobrious epithet for 'Jewish Bolshevism'

ŻZW   *Żydowski Związek Wojskowy* (Jewish Military Union, active in wartime Poland)

Acknowledgements

I have been discussing Polish history for longer than I care to remember, principally with my late father, Władysław Stachura, whose non-political but patriotic perspectives, honed during his service in the Polish Army from the first until the last day of the Second World War, have undoubtedly helped shape my own views.

More recently, I am grateful to the undergraduate students at the University of Stirling who have taken my third-year course, 'The Second Polish Republic, 1918–1939/45', for their often lively contributions in seminars.

Since its foundation in 1996, The Polish Society, of which I am Chairman, has provided a stimulating and convivial forum for further debate.

I am pleased to express my gratitude to the M. B. Grabowski Fund, London, for awarding The Polish Society a grant in aid of its academic publishing programme, of which this book is a part. The Chairman of the M. B. Grabowski Fund, Mr G. J. Palmi, is particularly thanked for his support for my work.

Peter D. Stachura
Bridge of Allan
Polish National Day, 3 May 1998

Introduction

The essays presented in this book have been written during the last few years. Most of them are now published for the first time, while two others, which have previously been published, have been revised and updated.[1] Altogether, this collection, in examining a variegated, interrelated menu of themes, aims to make an informative and stimulating statement about Poland's historical development from the beginning to the end of the twentieth century.

As anyone even remotely aware of the historiography of modern Polish history will know, there are numerous areas and topics which have been at the centre of often acrimonious debate, a considerable part of which has been influenced by political and ideological proclivities, particularly since 1945. The end result has been that Poland and her history have frequently been misrepresented, even denigrated. The period of the Second Republic perhaps provides the most salient example of this regrettable trend, for scholarly views of it in former Communist Poland and the West have been uniformly negative, to one degree or another. It is argued in the present volume, however, that this reputation is unjustified, as are some other criticisms of Poland's development this century. If my essays have one fundamental, unifying objective, it is to advance a more balanced and objective analysis of important subjects, thus to comprehend Polish history not simply in terms of the undoubted failures and disappointments, but also from a perspective which extends appropriate recognition of the achievements and successes within a broader context of a country and a people who are at once fascinating and admirable, if also exasperating and saddening.

The first essay examines what might be regarded as the theme that runs through all periods of modern Polish history, namely, the striving for and consolidation, loss and regaining of independence, all within a relatively brief period. This matter, although always shaped by Poland's unfortunate geographical location between two stronger and invariably hostile powers, Germany and Russia/the Soviet Union, has brought out the best and the worst

1

in Poles: heroic, unselfish and patriotic endeavour, which characterized the creation and consolidation of the Second Republic,
alongside fatalistic collaboration, factionalism and petty advan-
tage-seeking, as displayed most vividly during most of the
Communist era. A comprehensive examination follows of the
first era of national independence after the end of the First World
War, with a concern to acknowledge the limitations and weaknesses which so many commentators have repeatedly emphasized,
as well as Poland's accomplishments in a variety of important
fields, despite a multitude of significant domestic and external
obstacles. The Second Republic before the Second World War
was certainly no oasis of tranquillity and shining success in an
inter-war Europe scarred by profound economic, social and political instability, catastrophic failure and ascendant totalitarianism.
On an international scale of measurement, on the other hand,
the Republic had arguably far more to commend it than the
majority of its contemporaries, whether democratic or authoritarian, capitalist or socialist. This is why, after heroic defeat in the
September Campaign of 1939, Poles at home and abroad rallied
wholeheartedly on numerous battlefields across Europe behind
the cause of their nation's freedom and independence.

No attempt at coming to terms with modern Poland could be
complete or even merely adequate without reference to its substantial Jewish community. The appalling tragedy of the Holocaust,
the Third Reich's systematic extermination on Polish soil of
some six million Jews, half of them Polish citizens, inevitably
casts a deep shadow over any discussion of Polish–Jewish relations, a subject which has aroused more controversy and bitterness than almost any other to do with Polish history. Yet this
must not prevent a search for the truth of those relations, before,
during and after the war. Two of the essays here try to construct
as balanced and objective a picture as is possible at this juncture.

In the first instance, it is argued that the overall situation of the
more than three million Jews in pre-war Poland was not as disadvantageous as has usually been made out, and that despite an
undeniable and deplorable degree of anti-Semitism, especially
following the death of Marshal Józef Piłsudski in 1935, they
enjoyed wide freedoms, to such an extent that they constituted

the most vibrant and modernizing Jewish community in Europe. Moreover, the evidence indicates that their material standard of living was superior to that of their average Polish neighbour. This reality cannot easily be squared with the allegations of widespread discrimination, abuse and terror that colour so many narratives of their situation, which compared favourably with that of their fellow Jews in many other European countries at that time, especially in those where specific anti-Semitic legislation was enacted. The rarely mentioned subject of Jewish polonophobia must also find a place in the balance sheet, as should the equally ignored fact that many Poles were repelled by anti-Semitic manifestations of all kinds.

In any case, as is intimated in the second essay on Polish–Jewish relations, there can be no question of pre-war anti-Semitism in Poland having somehow prepared the way for the Holocaust, which must be ascribed to the vile, overpowering and all-encompassing racist dynamics of National Socialism. None the less, at the end of a war in which both Poles and Jews had experienced unprecedented, unimaginable suffering, their hatred for one another had indubitably reached new heights of intensity. The reasons are to be found in a number of wartime developments, including the anti-Polish activities of many Jews in Soviet-occupied Eastern Poland in 1939–41, the severe setbacks Free Poland had to endure, including the defeat of the Warsaw Uprising in 1944 and the arrant betrayal at Yalta the following year, and, not least, the imposition with Western connivance of an alien and detested ideological, political and economic system by the Soviet Union in which a small Jewish Communist élite wielded considerable power.

This utterly undeserved and depressing outcome in 1945 flew in the face of the valiant and important military contribution the Poles had made to the winning of the war against Hitler, epitomized by two outstanding personalities who are appraised within the broader framework of the inter-war and wartime periods, General Władysław Sikorski and General Stanisław Maczek. Sikorski, who had emerged a national hero from the Polish–Soviet War of 1919–20, and who had given additional sterling service to his country in the early 1920s as Prime Minister and

Minister of Defence before falling foul of Marshal Piłsudski, was by no means a unanimous choice in Autumn 1939 as leader of the Polish Government-in-Exile and Commander-in-Chief of the Polish Armed Forces. During his tenure of these offices until his death in 1943 he had to confront a good deal of opposition from within his own government, the largely Piłsudskiite army officer corps and the wider Polish émigré community in London. Sikorski's most formidable and ultimately destructive challenge, however, came from Poland's allies, Britain, the United States and, of course, the Soviet Union, all of whom had the military and political clout to marginalize and then finally ignore the cause of democratic freedom and national independence which he personified. Sikorski was guilty of crucial errors of judgement at certain times, especially as regards relations with the Soviets, while his trust in Churchill and his plan for a Central European Federation were rather naive and unrealistic. But he was not in a position to influence the broader Allied agenda, in which by the end of the war Free Poland hardly figured at all. None the less, although some of the myths surrounding Sikorski are dispelled in this essay, there is no denying his status as one of the most outstanding Polish leaders of modern times.

General Maczek, a career army officer since the beginning of the Second Republic, laid his claim to fame in two ways. The first was as Commander of the First Polish Armoured Division which, having been established in Scotland in 1942, proceeded to play a crucial part in the Normandy Campaign, above all at the Battle of the Falaise Gap in August 1944, which turned the tide decisively in the Allies' favour in that particular theatre. A stream of further resounding victories against stiff German opposition in Northern France and the Low Countries, culminating in the German surrender at Wilhelmshaven in early spring 1945, consolidated Maczek's reputation for dashing brilliance as well as that of his division as one of the finest and most successful military units of the entire Second World War. Secondly, Maczek emerged, from his home in Edinburgh, as the unofficial leader of the substantial exiled Polish community in Scotland after 1945, and was revered not least for his uncompromising repudiation of the Soviet-imposed Communist regime in his beloved homeland, to which he never returned. By the time of his death, in 1994, he had become a legend among Poles in Scotland and the world over.

The situation of the exiled Poles in Scotland is assessed in a further essay, which delineates the difficulties they faced in a post-war environment that was far from friendly or propitious. Betrayed finally at Yalta, the Poles gradually had to accept that their exile would be permanent in a Scotland where post-war austerity combined with political, trade unionist and sectarian animosity to produce an uneasy situation. In an environment that was in many respects the antithesis of pre-war Poland, the large majority of Poles still succeeded in maintaining their traditional customs and patriotic convictions within their own organizations, especially the Polish Ex-Combatants' Association (SPK), and were generally united in denouncing the Communist regime in Warsaw as illegitimate. Over time, not unnaturally, a process of limited assimilation was set in train. By the 1960s a second generation of Polish background was beginning to make its way, though not necessarily in full harmony with the older, wartime generation, whose numbers inevitably declined, thus accelerating assimilationist tendencies. Strong emotional ties to the idea of a Free Poland remained much in evidence, however, notably with the advent of a Polish Pope, the exhilarating rise of *Solidarność* and then the dramatic collapse of the Communist system in 1989/90. The contemporary Polish community in Scotland may be smaller than before, but it has managed to retain a certain vibrancy and develop greater self-confidence, which have allowed it to make a noteworthy contribution to wider society. Even so, its longer-term future remains uncertain in a Scotland whose own destiny as a nation is currently being avidly debated.

Picking up on the theme of post-Communist Poland, the final essay examines the content of Polish nationalism with reference to historical antecedents and possible future lines of development, which will be strongly influenced by Poland's growing re-approximation to the West through her transition to a free-market economy, membership of NATO and, most probably at a later date, of the European Union. With due regard for the significance of *Solidarność* as a patriotic movement of anti-Communist protest in the 1980s, as well as the enduring role of the Catholic Church as a symbol of 'Polishness', the difficulties confronting Poland in re-establishing a fully fledged national identity in the 1990s are reviewed, especially in relation to certain political parties, such as the nationalist Confederation for an Independent Poland (KPN). Finally, it is suggested that a refashioned and modernized Polish nationalism or patriotism, devoid of unpleasant aspects of its past, such as anti-Semitism, and based on a *modus vivendi* with its traditional enemies, Germany and Russia, can be a force for good in a Europe which no longer has the nefarious menace of Soviet Communism hovering over it.

NOTES

1.   'Władysław Sikorski: Soldier, Politician, Statesman, 1881–1943', was published in the *Scottish Slavonic Review*, 21 (1993, Autumn), pp. 71–94, and 'Polish Nationalism in the Post-Communist Era' appeared in J. Amodia (ed.), *The Resurgence of Nationalist Movements in Europe* (Bradford, 1993), pp. 96–109.

1 Poland's Independence: From Versailles to Yalta, and Beyond*

The theme of independence lies at the very heart of Poland's historical development from the eighteenth century until the present day. This theme might be said, indeed, to be a veritable barometer of Poland's situation at any given moment, and arguably more than any other factor has influenced the Poles' own relationship with and understanding of their country, and the perception of Poland that foreign observers have formed over time.

The independence of Poland was proclaimed in Warsaw on 11 November 1918, with Józef Piłsudski, who had arrived in the capital only the previous day following his release from German captivity, as the putative Head of State. Thus ended over one hundred years of partition and repression. Although the so-called 'Polish Question' had been intermittently part of the agenda of international diplomacy during the nineteenth century, Poland had ceased to exist as a political entity – until now.

The regaining of national independence has been derided by some historians because they believe that the Poles themselves contributed little to the process.[1] It is true, of course, that without the wider context of the First World War and the profound upheavals it brought in its train, there would have been little or no chance of the 'Polish Question', or any other, being resolved in a satisfactory manner. In particular, the collapse of the three imperial powers, Russia, Germany and Austria–Hungary, which had partitioned Poland, and the assertion of the principle of national self-determination by President Woodrow Wilson of the United States, created the opportunity for momentous change. In Poland's case, that opportunity was seized and brought to a successful conclusion largely by the efforts of the Poles themselves, which may be delineated as follows.

First, the Polish insurrections against Russian oppression in 1830–31 and 1863–4 were heroic failures, and terminated the era of Romantic Nationalism in Poland that had inspired them. But the struggle for freedom continued in a different fashion, initially, after 1863, through the process usually referred to as 'Organic Work'. Influenced philosophically by Warsaw Positivism, this process involved a conscious effort to develop the economy and institutions in Poland in preparation for a future state of independence. The Polish language, culture and civilization were to be cherished in order to maintain Polish national identity in the face of the brutal and sweeping policies of Russification and Germanization that were unleashed during the course of the second half of the nineteenth century. This movement for national salvation was generally successful.[2]

Second, there was the revival in the later decades of the nineteenth century of the tradition of idealism, and with it of a reinvigorated Polish national consciousness in society as a whole, that is, including the peasantry for the first time, as part of a broader development of a more militant form of nationalism that swept across Europe.[3] In Poland this new wave of nationalism was given the most muscular political expression by the National Democratic Party under the leadership of Roman Dmowski. Through its limited representation in the *Duma*, the Russian parliament set up by the Tsar shortly after the 1905 Revolution to help appease his liberal critics, it aimed to secure autonomy for Poland within the Tsarist Empire as a stepping-stone to full independence in the longer term.[4]

Third, even before the advent of the National Democrats, the torch of Polish nationalism combined with revolutionary Socialism had been carried by the Polish Socialist Party (PPS) in Russian Poland. This militant organization, dedicated to the overthrow of the Tsarist autocracy by force of arms, was of peculiar significance for the cause of Polish independence because it was subsequently led by Józef Piłsudski.[5] Before the end of the century, therefore, the two personalities who were destined to make the most substantive personal contribution to the struggle for independence, and also to the development of the Second Polish Republic after 1918, were already conspicuously, though separately, active on the scene: Roman Dmowski and Józef Piłsudski.

Fourth, during the First World War the specific Polish input to the struggle for independence came in both military and politico-diplomatic spheres, though not necessarily in a coordinated fashion: for example, there were the famous Legions created and led by Piłsudski, General Haller's Polish Army in France and the *Polnische Wehrmacht*, and then Dmowski through the Polish National Committee (KNP) in 1917–19, as well as the networking of Ignacy Paderewski in the American 'corridors of power'.[6]

These contributions ensured that the 'Polish Question' would finally emerge by the end of the war, despite serious obstacles, at the top of the diplomatic agenda. Unsurprisingly, there was opposition to this from Russia and Germany, who had both advanced hastily conceived and intrinsically spurious autonomy plans for Poland: but opposition came also from Britain, who argued against Polish independence until a very late date in the war. For political and personal reasons, Prime Minister David Lloyd George was no friend of Poland, then or later.[7]

Furthermore, it has to be acknowledged that the strong, well-organized 'Jewish lobby' at the Paris Peace Conference in 1919 fought desperately to prevent the creation of an independent Polish state. When that failed, this powerful pressure group secured the Minorities Treaty, which was actually designed to safeguard the rights and interests of the large Jewish communities in the new states of East–Central Europe, but with Poland especially in mind. It proved to be a Pyrrhic victory, for the Poles deeply resented having this Treaty thrust upon them as an integral part of the peace settlement, viewing it, understandably, as both unnecessary and as a blatant infringement of Poland's newly won sovereignty.[8]

The final outcome of the peace negotiations, the Republic of Poland, was thus no 'fluke' but rather the result of historical events shaped by both Poles and non-Poles, the one indispensably complementing the other. Independence had been achieved only after a prolonged, hard struggle: retaining it in an unstable and hostile Europe would prove to be an even more formidable challenge, particularly when it soon became clear that the future of the Polish state, formally created by the Treaty of Versailles in June 1919, lay almost entirely in its own hands, notwithstanding the alliance with France in 1921.

Poland was immediately confronted by a host of external and internal dangers which threatened to abort it: not only a multitude of the most dire economic, financial, social and institutional problems, many of which were part of the original partitionist legacy,[9] but also the bitter enmity of Weimar Germany and what was now Soviet Russia, seemed certain to overwhelm the nascent Republic. During the first few years of her existence Poland had to fight no fewer than six wars, including, most notably, against the Soviet Bolsheviks, in order to assert her territorial integrity. The situation in the East was especially fluid, as the peacemakers at the Paris conference had deliberately left that issue unresolved, while the British offer of what became known as the 'Curzon Line' was patently unacceptable to the Poles. The Polish Army's famous victory, under the leadership of Marshal Piłsudski, over the Red Army at the gates of Warsaw in August 1920 proved to be a decisive turning-point,[10] inspiring Poland to settle other territorial disputes on reasonably favourable terms. By 1922–3 her borders had been comprehensively settled and internationally recognized.

During these early years also, however, the independence of the Polish Republic had been seriously threatened from within from two directions. First, there were the ethnic minorities – the large numbers of Germans, Ukrainians, Belorussians and Jews – comprising about one-third of the total population, and their political parties, which generally failed to play a constructive role in developing Poland's system of parliamentary democracy. Many members of these ethnic groups resented being citizens of the Polish state, despite their enjoyment of a diverse range of freedoms in their economic, social, cultural, religious and political life.[11] Second, a threat existed from the Poles themselves, as a result of bitter internecine squabbling, especially between the nationalist Right (*Endecja*) and the Piłsudski camps. The lack of political experience and maturity on the part of both the political class and the electorate meant that the early and mid-1920s were characterized by frequent change of cabinet, scandal, graft and corruption, all of which discredited and rendered largely ineffective the governmental system. By 1926, Marshal Piłsudski, who had retired in disgust from political life a few years previously, concluded that the instability of the political system was so fundamental that he believed Poland's independence was once more being placed in serious jeopardy. To preserve it, and at the same time no doubt to assert his own personal priorities, he staged his successful *coup d'état* in May of that year.[12]

The era of the *Sanacja*, the term given to the new regime headed by Piłsudski, which extended beyond the Marshal's death in 1935 until the outbreak of the Second World War, is rather controversial in Polish historiography. Whatever may be said of it, however, there is no denying that Poland's status as an independent state was now in relatively safer hands, despite the ravages of the Depression in the 1930s. The extravagances of the earlier parliamentary system were curtailed within an increasingly authoritarian framework, which owed much to Piłsudski's charismatic stature and influence.[13] On the other hand, during this time Europe as a whole, and Poland in particular, experienced the lengthening, aggressive shadows of both Stalinism and National Socialism, which boded ill for the future.

Despite concluding Non-Aggression Pacts with these two neighbours, in 1932 with the Soviet Union and in 1934 with Germany, Poland's position was inevitably becoming less and less secure. Her room for manoeuvre was, in any event, circumscribed by the changing balance in international relations to the detriment of Britain and France. Piłsudski was all too painfully aware of this change, particularly as he expected no help from Britain and precious little from an increasingly debilitated Third French Republic, and was convinced that before too long his ambitious 'Doctrine of the Two Enemies' would run its natural course, leaving Poland to fight again to preserve her independence.[14]

Throughout the inter-war period in general, Poland, despite her best efforts, found it impossible to anchor her independence in comfortable security. Her position was inherently precarious, especially as the Soviet Union and Germany were determined to regain what had been lost in 1918–20. The Soviets, as imperialist

under the cloak of revolutionary Bolshevism as their Tsarist pre-
decessors, were never reconciled to the existence of Poland as an
independent state, and sought revenge, moreover, for their humiliating defeat in the war of 1919–20. For their part, the Germans,
even during the Stresemann era of peace and cooperation with
the West in the mid-1920s (*Erfüllungspolitik*), which resulted in
the Locarno Pact and Germany's admittance to the League of
Nations, never gave up on the 'lost' eastern territories, and constantly sought to undermine Poland by all possible diplomatic
and economic means (for instance, through the Tariff War of
1925–34).[15] After all, they continued to adhere to their traditional
view of Poland being a '*Saisonstaat*' – here today and gone
tomorrow. Hitler had intimated in *Mein Kampf* his long-term
objective of realizing *Lebensraum*,[16] an updated version of the
post-Bismarckian policy of eastward expansion (*Drang nach
Osten*), as revealed in the Treaty of Brest–Litovsk with defeated
Russia in March 1918. Poland was their common enemy, which
they were resolved to destroy when the circumstances were right.
The infamous Hitler–Stalin Pact in August 1939 created those
very circumstances.

The September Campaign of 1939, the prelude to defeat and
genocidal occupation by both the Nazis and Soviets,[17] closed the
latest chapter of Polish independence, though, as before, not the
ambition of the Poles to regain it. The Polish Government-in-
Exile, led from 1939 until his death in 1943 by General
Władysław Sikorski, bore the major responsibility in this respect.
Tragically, it was always destined to play a secondary role in
Allied government circles, above all once the Soviet Union, itself
invaded in June 1941 by its erstwhile ally, Germany, was welcomed as a partner in the Grand Alliance. It is clear in retrospect
that the United States and Britain, however much their leaders
may have admired General Sikorski personally, were prepared
from the outset to cynically sacrifice his government and the
Polish national interest that it embodied in order to please Stalin
and thus keep him as an ally.[18]

1943 was a crucial year for Poland's already rapidly declining
status and influence with the Western Allies. Stalin's victories at
Stalingrad, and then Kursk, turned the tide on the Eastern Front

irrevocably in his favour, making it more imperative than ever, in the Allies' eyes, to keep him on their side, for there was always a fear that having lined up together once Stalin and Hitler were eminently capable of doing so again: was a nightmare scenario which Churchill and Roosevelt were desperate to avoid at all costs. This was made abundantly obvious when the Katyń Affair, uncovered in April 1943, was not allowed to distrub their relations with Stalin, despite his abrupt breaking off of diplomatic relations with the Sikorski government when it demanded an independent enquiry into the Katyń murders by the International Red Cross.[19]

Sikorski's death several months later was, of course, a further, indeed fatal, blow to the Polish cause, because it removed from the scene a personality of genuine stature who was not adequately replaced.[20] Even so, it has to be said that quite some time before the General's death Poland had completely lost the political battle with the Allies, and there was nothing that anyone on the Polish side could do about it. At the Tehran Conference in December, to which, significantly, Polish officials were not invited. Churchill and Roosevelt agreed to give their ally, Stalin, a more or less free hand in Poland. In practice that meant the inevitable annexation by the Soviet Union of the Eastern provinces, or about 40 per cent of the territory of the pre-war Polish Republic, and the imposition of Soviet Communism in Poland at the end of the war.

Consequently, and notwithstanding the substantial Polish military contribution to the triumphant Allied war effort in 1944–5, which included the victories of General Władysław Anders and his Second Corps at Monte Cassino, and of General Stanisław Maczek and the First Armoured Division in Normandy and the Low Countries and, in addition, the valiant if doomed Warsaw Uprising by the Home Army (AK),[21] Poland had been effectively lost, with Western connivance.

The Yalta Conference in early 1945 merely confirmed this appalling, utterly undeserved outcome of political and diplomatic defeat amidst military victory. Even more than 50 years after this event, its grotesque unfairness, duplicity and sheer crassness is impossible to comprehend or accept.[22] Poland's 'reward' for her faithful and considerable role in the defeat of Hitler's Germany was half a century of Communism which, before the war, had only an exiguous following in the country.[23] Mass deportations to the Gulags,[24] wholesale murder, base moral and spiritual standards, economic exploitation and ruin, and loss of independence and sovereignty lay ahead for Poland, now transformed into an abject Soviet satellite.[25] How Marshal Piłsudski, conqueror of the Soviet Bolsheviks only a quarter of a century previously, must have turned in his grave!

Thankfully, however, nothing is for ever, and throughout that dark Communist epoch there were those who managed to keep the flame of national independence flickering. Not only the continuing oppositional activity of the Polish Government-in-Exile in London, but also, above all, the rise of *Solidarność* and the election in 1978 of a patriotic Polish Pope, probably did more than anything else to advance the cause. Admittedly, though, the intrinsic evil and corruption of the Communist system in Poland also had to bring its own nemesis.[26]

The events of 1989/90 constituted yet another episode in the ongoing drama that is modern Poland. Independence was re-established, the Communists were discredited and swept out of power, the Red Army was soon on its way home, and Poland began to re-enter the Western World where she belongs. Such excitement! What had been dreamt of all those years, especially by those Poles who had refused as a matter of patriotic principle to return after the war to a Communist Poland, had at last been realized, though many, regrettably, had not lived to savour the day of victory.

Can this really be said to be the final chapter in the saga of Polish independence? Can it ever again be lost? Have the Russians really gone away for good? Have the Germans also gone away? No-one can be certain, particularly in view of the sobering fact that within a mere three years or so of independence being regained the Polish electorate voted into office a government dominated by 'former', or perhaps 'reformed', Communists.[27] Furthermore, this development was no aberration, for a few years later the same electorate voted as President of Poland a former Communist Party apparatchik.[28] Is Poland now the

'Second People's Republic', or the 'Third Polish Republic'? The confusion over her true identity is profound.[29]

Clearly, many imponderables remain in the present situation. It can only be hoped that all the heroic endeavour in the cause of independence over the last two centuries will not end, once again, in tears. And, as before, the threat to independence may not be confined to Poland's external enemies alone. Above all, the nefarious activities of the small band of Polish Communists in 1944–5 and subsequently on behalf of its Soviet masters should act as a salutary warning.[30]

NOTES

*This is the slightly extended version of a Paper delivered to a meeting of The Polish Society that was held at the University of Glasgow on 11 November 1996. I am grateful to several members of the Society for their comments.

1. N. Davies. *God's Playground: A History of Poland, Volume II: 1795 to the Present* (Oxford, 1982), p. 392.
2. P. S. Wandycz, *The Lands of Partitioned Poland, 1795–1918* (Seattle, London, 1984), pp. 193–272; S. B. Blejwas, *Realism in Polish Politics: Warsaw Positivism and National Survival in Nineteenth Century Poland* (New Haven, 1984); W. W. Hagan, 'National Solidarity and Organic Work in Prussian Poland, 1815–1914', *Journal of Modern History*, 44 (1972), No. 1, pp. 38–64; T. R. Weeks, 'Defining Us and Them: Poles and Russians in the Western Provinces, 1863–1914', *Slavic Review*, 53 (1994), No. 1, pp. 26–40.
3. See S. Kieniewicz, *The Emancipation of the Polish Peasantry* (Chicago, 1969); and O. A. Narkiewicz, *The Green Flag: Polish Populist Politics, 1867–1970* (London, 1970).
4. E. Chmielewski, *The Polish Question in the Russian State Duma* (Knoxsville, Tenn., 1970); A. M. Fountain. *Roman Dmowski: Party, Tactics, Ideology 1895–1907* (Boulder, Col., 1980); R. E. Blobaum. *Rewolucja: Russian Poland, 1904–1907* (Ithaca, New York, 1995); B. A. Porter, 'Who is a Pole and Where is Poland? Territory and Nation in the Rhetoric of Polish National Democracy before 1905', *Slavic Review*, 51 (1992), No. 4. pp. 639–53.
5. L. Blit, *The Origins of Polish Socialism: The History and Ideas of the First Polish Socialist Party, 1878–1886* (London, 1971); R. E. Blobaum, *Feliks Dzierzyński and the SDKPiL. A Study of the Origins of Polish Communism* (Boulder, Col., 1984).

6. Still useful, despite signs of ageing, is T. Komarnicki, *The Rebirth of the Polish Republic: A Study in the Diplomatic History of Europe, 1914–1920* (London, 1957); see also G. J. Lerski, 'Dmowski, Paderewski and American Jews', *Polin*, 2 (1987), pp. 95–116.
7. N. Davies, 'Lloyd George and Poland, 1919–20', *Journal of Contemporary History*, 6 (1971), No. 1, pp. 132–54.
8. K. Lundgreen-Nielsen, *The Polish Problem at the Paris Peace Conference: A Study of the Policies of the Great Powers and the Poles, 1918–1919* (Odense, 1979); E. C. Black, 'Lucien Wolf and the Making of Poland, Paris 1919', *Polin*, 2 (1987), pp. 5–36; M. Levene, 'Nationalism and its Alternatives in the International Arena: The Jewish Question at Paris, 1919', *Journal of Contemporary History*, 28 (1993), No. 3, pp. 511–31; M. Levene, *War, Jews and the New Europe. The Diplomacy of Lucien Wolf, 1914–1919* (Oxford, 1992); I. Lewin and N. M. Gelber, *A History of Polish Jewry during the Renewal of Poland* (New York, 1990).
9. Z. Landau and J. Tomaszewski, *The Polish Economy in the Twentieth Century* (London, 1985); P. Latawski (ed.), *The Reconstruction of Poland, 1914–1923* (London, 1992).
10. Detailed coverage in N. Davies, *White Eagle, Red Star: The Polish–Soviet War, 1919–20* (London, 1972), esp. pp. 188–225; A. Zamoyski, *The Battle of the Marchlands* (Boulder, Col., 1981), pp. 125–40; M. K. Dziewanowski, *Joseph Piłsudski: A European Federalist, 1918–22* (Stanford, 1969).
11. The scholarly literature on this sensitive topic is generally unsatisfactory because of rather blatant anti-Polish bias. The tone was set by S. Horak, *Poland and her National Minorities, 1919–39* (New York, 1961), and has been continued by, for example, M. M. Drozdowski, 'The National Minorities in Poland in 1918–1939', *Acta Poloniae Historica*, 22 (1970), pp. 226–51; B. Budurowycz, 'Poland and the Ukrainian Problem, 1921–1939', *Canadian Slavic Papers*, 25 (1983), No. 4, pp. 473–500; R. Blanke, *Orphans of Versailles: The Germans in Western Poland, 1918–1939* (Lexington, Kentucky, 1993); and M. Palij, *The Ukrainian–Polish Defensive Alliance, 1919–1921. An Aspect of the Ukrainian Revolution* (Toronto, 1995). The most balanced survey is one of the earliest, A. Żółtowski, *Border of Europe: A Study of the Polish Eastern Provinces* (London, 1950). Polish–Jewish relations is, of course, a particularly controversial subject, on which the literature often reaches new depths of anti-Polish prejudice: for example, in J. Marcus, *Social and Political History of the Jews in Poland, 1919–1939* (New York, 1983), and C. S. Heller, *On the Edge of Destruction: Jews of Poland Between the Two World Wars* (New York, 1977). In a more recent volume, Y. Gutman *et al.* (eds), *The Jews of Poland Between Two World Wars* (Hanover, New England, 1989), there is at least an attempt by several contributors to apply a more informed perspective. Unfortunately, however, many articles in the journal *Polin* are somewhat tendentious.

12. J. Rothschild, *Piłsudski's Coup d'Etat* (New York, 1966); background provided by A. Polonsky, *Politics in Independent Poland, 1920–1939: The Crisis of Constitutional Government* (Oxford, 1972); R. F. Leslie (ed.), *The History of Poland since 1863* (London, 1983), pp. 139–58.

13. Biographies (in English) worth consulting are W. F. Reddaway, *Marshal Piłsudski* (London, 1939); W. Jędrzejewicz, *Piłsudski. A Life for Poland* (New York, 1982); A. Garlicki, *Józef Piłsudski, 1867–1935* (New York, 1995).

14. Jędrzejewicz, *op.cit.*, p. 305 ff.

15. From the extensive literature, see especially A. M. Cienciala, *From Versailles to Locarno: Keys to Polish Foreign Policy, 1919–1925* (Lawrence, Kansas, 1984); R. Debicki, *The Foreign Policy of Poland, 1919–1939* (New York, 1962); J. Karski, *The Great Powers and Poland, 1919–1945: From Versailles to Yalta* (New York, 1985); J. Korbel, *Poland Between East and West: Soviet and German Diplomacy towards Poland, 1919–1933* (Princeton, 1963); A. Korczyński and S. Świętochowski (eds), *Poland Between Germany and Russia, 1926–1939* (New York, 1975); H. von Riekhoff, *German–Polish Relations, 1918–1933* (Baltimore, 1971); P. S. Wandycz, *Soviet–Polish Relations, 1917–1921* (Cambridge, Mass., 1969).

16. A. Hitler, *Mein Kampf* (English edition, London, 1969), pp. 586–609.

17. For a general survey, see J. Garliński, *Poland in the Second World War* (London, 1985). More specific are J. T. Gross, *Polish Society under German Occupation: The Generalgouvernement, 1939–1944* (Princeton, 1979); J. T. Gross, *Revolution from Abroad: The Soviet Conquest of Poland's Western Ukraine and Western Byelorussia* (Princeton, 1988); S. Korboński, *The Polish Underground State: A Guide to the Underground, 1939–1945* (Boulder, Col., 1978); R. C. Lukas, *The Forgotten Holocaust: The Poles under German Occupation, 1939–1944* (Lexington, Kentucky, 1986); K. Sword (ed.), *The Soviet Takeover of the Polish Eastern Provinces, 1939–41* (London, 1991).

18. Developments are usefully covered by, for example, A. Polonsky (ed.), *The Great Powers and the Polish Question, 1941–1945* (London, 1976); S. M. Miner, *Between Churchill and Stalin: The Soviet Union, Great Britain and the Origins of the Grand Alliance* (London, 1990); G. V. Kacewicz, *Great Britain, the Soviet Union, and the Polish Government-in-Exile (1939–1945)* (The Hague, 1979); and S. Zochowski, *British Policy in Relation to Poland in the Second World War* (New York, 1988). More problematic are M. Kitchen, *British Policy Towards the Soviet Union during the Second World War* (London, 1986), and A. J. Prażmowska, *Britain and Poland, 1939–1943. The Betrayed Ally* (Cambridge, 1995). For relevant documents, see Sikorski Historical Institute, *Documents on Polish–Soviet Relations, 1939–1945* (London, 1961).

19. J. K. Zawodny, *Death in the Forest: The Story of the Katyń Massacre* (London, 1971); Polish Cultural Foundation, *The Crime of Katyń: Facts and Documents* (London, 1965).

20. K. Sword (ed.), *Sikorski: Soldier and Statesman* (London, 1990); P. D. Stachura, 'Władysław Sikorski: Soldier, Politician, Statesman, 1881–1943', *Scottish Slavonic Review*, 21 (1993), Autumn, pp. 71–94.

21. A judicious summary is given by A. Suchcitz, *Poland's Contribution to the Allied Victory in the Second World War* (London, 1995). See also J. K. Zawodny, *Nothing but Honour: The Story of the Warsaw Uprising* (London, 1978); A. Chmielarz, 'Warsaw Fought Alone: Reflections on Aid to and the Fall of the 1944 Uprising', *The Polish Review*, 39 (1994), No. 4, pp. 415–33. To be treated sceptically is J. M. Ciechanowski, *The Warsaw Rising of 1994* (London, 1974), for it contains too many distorted arguments.

22. A valuable source is Z. C. Szkopiak (ed.), *The Yalta Agreements: Documents prior to, during and after the Crimea Conference, 1945* (London, 1986), esp. pp. 30–48, 51–147. Further, A. M. Cienciala, 'Great Britain and Poland Before and After Yalta (1943–1945): A Reassessment', *The Polish Review*, 40 (1995), No. 3, pp. 281–313; W. Larsh, 'Yalta and the American Approach to Free Elections in Poland', *The Polish Review*, 40 (1995), No. 3, pp. 267–80.

23. A broad overview of the Polish Communists is given in M. K. Dziewanowski, *The Communist Party of Poland: An Outline of its History* (Cambridge, Mass., 1976), and J. B. de Weydenthal, *The Communists of Poland: An Historical Outline* (Stanford, 1978). More detailed and particular accounts are J. Schatz, *The Generation: The Rise and Fall of the Jewish Communists of Poland* (Berkeley, Cal., 1991), and T. Szafer, 'The Origins of the Communist Party in Poland, 1918–1921', in I. Banac (ed.), *The Effects of World War I. The Class War after the Great War. The Rise of Communist Parties in East Central Europe, 1918–1921* (New York, 1983), pp. 5–52.

24. K. Sword, *Deportation and Exile: Poles in the Soviet Union, 1939–48* (London, 1994) is an important, pioneering study. See also G. C. Malcher, *Blank Pages: Soviet Genocide against the Polish People* (Woking, 1993).

25. Documentary evidence is in A. Polonsky and B. Drukier, *The Beginnings of Communist Rule in Poland, December 1943 – June 1945* (London, 1980). For general background, see K. Kersten, *The Establishment of Communist Rule in Poland, 1943–1948* (London, 1993); and still useful is S. Mikołajczyk, *The Rape of Poland: The Pattern of Soviet Domination* (New York, 1948).

26. Among the better accounts are T. Garton Ash, *The Polish Revolution* (London, 1983), and L. Weschler, *The Passion of Poland: From Solidarity through to the State of War* (New York, 1984). Lech Wałęsa, *A Path of Hope: An Autobiography* (London, 1987), pp. 93–243, provides relatively few original insights. Similarly, the newly published memoirs of Pope John II, *Gift and Mystery* (New York, 1996), reveal very little, if anything, about his role in the collapse of Communism.

27. Reports in *The Times*, 19 September and 21 September, 1993.

28. Report by Robert Boyes in *The Times*, 21 November, 1995.

29. Since the Communist-dominated government took over in Autumn 1993, it has launched, on the evidence available to the Polish community in Scotland (Glasgow and Edinburgh, at any rate), a concerted campaign to unite Polish organisations that had owed allegiance to the Polish Government-in-Exile with those Poles or groups who had worked or sympathised with the pre- 1989 Warsaw regime. Is this 'United Front' policy, reminiscent of the early post-war years in Poland, a prelude to a 'Red' takeover of these organisations?

30. In this respect T. Torańska, *'Them': Stalin's Polish Puppets* (New York, 1987), is poignantly instructive.

2 The Second Republic: A Historical Overview

The re-establishment of an independent and sovereign Polish state in November 1918, the Second Republic, capped the endeavours of the Polish nation to terminate the injustices and repression of the Partitionist Era which it had endured for 123 years. The quest for national liberation had assumed various forms, most notably the insurrections of 1830–31 and 1863–4 against the Russians, the Positivist-inspired period of 'Organic Work', and, in the latter decades of the nineteenth century, the separate strategies of revolutionary Socialism under Józef Piłsudski and of nationalism under the National Democratic Party of Roman Dmowski.[1] The outbreak of the First World War in 1914 opened up unforeseen and unprecedented opportunities for a successful resolution of the 'Polish Question', which had effectively disappeared from the agenda of international diplomacy in the second half of the century.

The involvement on opposing sides in the war of the partitionist powers, Tsarist Russia, Wilhelmine Germany and the Habsburg Empire, allowed the Poles to exploit, within certain limitations, the rapidly changing circumstances of the conflict to their advantage. If the Polish Legions epitomized the wider military contribution now made by the Poles, it was complemented by the diplomatic initiatives spearheaded by the Polish National Committee (KNP) in the corridors of Allied power. At various moments during the war the partitionist empires announced vague and half-hearted plans for granting the Poles some degree of autonomy in return for their help in the war. But the most significant development for the Polish cause came in 1917–18 from the overthrow of the Russian autocracy and the subsequent Bolshevik Revolution, and from the resolve of President Woodrow Wilson of the United States, articulated in his famous Fourteen Points of January 1918, to establish the principle of national self-determination as the bedrock of the peace settlement at the end of the war.[2] Moreover, the defeat of the Central Powers in Autumn 1918 created a vacuum

in the heart of Europe which was filled, according to the Paris
Peace Conference and the ensuing Treaty of Versailles in June
1919, by the creation of the so-called 'Successor States', of which
Poland was undeniably the most important. But the Polish contribution to the attainment of independence was both necessary and
substantial, contrary to the view that the events of November 1918
were 'a fluke', in which 'the wishes and actions of the Polish population were, to the very last moment, largely irrelevant'.[3]

The post-1945 historiography of the Second Republic has generally been highly critical, and on occasion denunciatory. Soviet
and Communist historians in 'People's Poland', especially during
the Stalinist era, set the tone by voicing scathing criticism of
its 'reactionary', 'militarist', 'capitalist' and 'clerical' nature, and
were often prepared to falsify or fabricate the historical evidence
to justify their opinions. This antipathy was readily endorsed by
left-wing and pro-Zionist scholars in the West, who added that the
Second Republic had also been virulently anti-Semitic and oppres-
sive towards its large ethnic minorities. Only during the slightly
more relaxed 1970s and 1980s in Poland were the ideological and
political imperatives behind historical scholarship somewhat less
apparent. Even then, however, too many works continued to bear
the hallmarks of Marxist–Leninist thinking and consequently had
to be treated carefully in respect of their interpretative analysis and
factual reliability.[4] None the less, Western observers of independent reputation have also invariably provided a negative assessment of the Second Republic. Perhaps the most prominent of
them has written that it was 'destined to destruction' because of
unresolved major domestic and external issues,[5] while another
describes inter-war Poland's history as 'indeed disheartening' on
account of 'signal failures' in important spheres.[6] Any praise that
has been afforded is usually limited or marginalized, and anyone
brave enough to swim against this tide of condemnation by
defending the Republic or underlining what they have considered
to have been positive aspects of its development is liable to be castigated as ill-informed, mischievous or arrantly nationalistic.[7]

It is clear that the Second Republic has aroused passionate
and controversial discussion, but it is surely axiomatic that any
assessment of it should take account not only of its undoubted

weaknesses and failures, but also its invariably unacknowledged or disparaged achievements.

Poland was the largest of the new states created in East-Central Europe after 1918, and the sixth largest, in terms of geographical area and population, in Europe as a whole. The national census of September 1921 recorded an area of 389,000 square kilometres and 27.2 million inhabitants, a figure which had risen to 32 million by the 1931 census, and to just over 35 million on the eve of the Second World War. The country remained overwhelmingly rural and agrarian in character throughout the period: in 1921 24 per cent of the population resided in towns and cities, increasing to only 30 per cent in 1939.[8]

From the perspective of November 1918 the longer-term chances of survival of the Republic appeared to be extraordinarily poor, despite the understandable wave of patriotic euphoria that swept through the nation as independence became a reality. In fact Poland had been reborn in the most inauspicious environment imaginable; 1918 may be regarded as her 'Year Zero', when a host of fundamental problems at home and abroad had to be tackled.

From abroad, she had to contend immediately with the searing animosity of Russia and Germany, at whose expense her independence had been largely won. Both these countries adopted a radically revisionist attitude towards the Treaty of Versailles and a specifically revanchist stance towards Poland, their mutual enemy, whom they vowed to destroy at the earliest possible opportunity. Subsequently vilified by the Russians as the 'bastard of Versailles' and as a *Saisonstaat*, an ephemeral entity, by the Germans,[9] Poland was made to feel permanently insecure. General Hans von Seeckt, Commander-in-Chief of the German Army (*Reichswehr*), made the revealing comment in September 1922:[10]

> Poland's existence is intolerable, at variance with the survival of Germany. It must disappear, and it will disappear through its own internal weakness and through Russia – with our assistance. For Russia, Poland is even more intolerable than for us; no Russian can allow Poland to exist. ... The creation of the broad common frontier between Russia and Germany is the precondition for the regaining of the strength of both countries.

The ostensible ideological incompatibility between the democratic Weimar Republic and Bolshevik Russia proved no obstacle to their conclusion in 1922 of a formal alliance with significant military implications, the Treaty of Rapallo, a crucial aspect of which was the aim of undermining Poland.[11] Furthermore, a good deal of hostility was directed at Poland from influential political and intellectual sources in the West, particularly from Jewish organizations in the United States and from Britain, who until a late stage in the war had been opposed to the very idea of an independent Polish state. After 1918, when Britain was concerned to secure a balance of interests on the continent, which meant curbing French ambitions – and to revive the European economy, which required the regeneration of Germany – leading personalities, including Prime Minister David Lloyd George, economist John Maynard Keynes, leading diplomat Sir James Headlam-Morley, and historians and political commentators Lewis Namier, E. H. Carr and Christopher Hill, were all united in their strident condemnation of Poland for her alleged imperialist agenda in the East, in Pomerania and Silesia, and for her alleged widespread anti-Semitism. As the United States retreated into isolationism only France (mainly for her own security reasons), Romania and Hungary displayed a friendly disposition towards the Poles.[12]

On the domestic front the challenges seemed no less daunting. The economic backwardness which still remained from the partitionist era, especially in Russian and Austrian Poland, combined with the devastation caused by the many battles of the First World War that had taken place on Polish soil and the systematic plundering and sabotage of maurauding armies, meant that the economy had to be rebuilt virtually from the lowest point. Millions of destroyed farms, homes and livestock had to be made good, along with the overnight loss of the Russian market. Except in the former German areas, agriculture was organized in a rather primitive fashion. Mechanization hardly existed, farms were generally less than twelve acres in size and geared only to subsistence levels, while over the twenty years of independence Poland's considerable increase in population was concentrated in the countryside, thus compounding major problems. Large-scale land reform was clearly an urgent requirement, but any attempt at modernization faced formidable barriers not least from the landowning aristocracy and its political allies, who feared the consequences of any weakening of the Polish landowning class in the Eastern Provinces.[13] Besides, the 1921 Constitution had explicitly guaranteed the rights of private property.

Poland's small and underdeveloped industrial and commercial sectors were based on textiles, especially in Łódź, coal-mining, salt and timber, and the small oilfields in Galicia. Other industrial centres of note were around Warsaw, the Drobina Basin, Upper Silesia and Częstochowa. Capital for investment was scarce, with little prospect of attracting it from abroad at anything other than exorbitant interest rates, and an indigeneous entrepreneurial class hardly existed alongside the predominant Jews and Germans. Part of the problem in this latter respect was the profound anti-industrial prejudice in Polish society, especially on the political Right. Moreover, the currency situation was chaotic, with no fewer than six separate currencies circulating in different parts of the country in these earliest years; and, of course, there was no central bank to provide even a semblance of stability in the embryonic financial and insurance systems. The creation of a modern fiscal system was another priority, especially as until 1923/4 government expenditure outstripped tax receipts by a ratio of 10 to 1, a certain recipe for serious inflation. To make the situation worse, only the mere rudiments of a transportation and communications network existed. Poland had relatively few roads, bridges or rolling stock, and the railways had different gauges. It is not surprising that government felt compelled to introduce a series of social reforms in an attempt to alleviate the worst effects of mass unemployment and other problems which arose from the economic and political vicissitudes of 1918–19. In short, the overall economic position of the country could not have been more unpropitious, or the challenge of reconstruction more demanding.

Amidst these economic problems, Poland was faced with the equally onerous task of integrating her large number of ethnic minorities into the state.[14] Poland was a multinational and multi-confessional state. According to the censuses of 1921 and 1931, approximately 30 per cent of the population was not ethnically

Polish, and substantial numbers of them resented being citizens of a Polish state in the first place. Above all, this was true of the five million Ukrainians in the south-eastern provinces, some of whom resorted to acts of terrorism, the almost one million Germans, mainly in western Poland, who later became enthusiastic followers of Adolf Hitler,[15] and the over three million Jews, representing 10 per cent of the whole population, who were more widely scattered, though most of them were resident in large towns or cities, or in small towns in Eastern Poland.[16] Their signal presence in industry, commerce, banking, small manufacturing and some liberal professions, as well as their distinctive religion, language (Yiddish and Hebrew), culture, dress and customs marked them out, the small percentage of assimilated Jews apart, as a conspicuous and resented community, particularly as many of them had been opposed to the establishment of Poland as an independent state,[17] and had supported or sympathized with Soviet Russia in its war with Poland in 1919–20.[18] Their loyalty thereafter was widely questioned. Finally, there were, in addition, 1.5 million Byelorussians in the north-east, and much smaller numbers of Russians, Tartars, Lithuanians and Czechs.

It was obviously in the best interests of the state and of the minorities themselves to find a way of living in harmony together. If total integration was not possible, then at least a *modus vivendi* had to be reached. The task had not been helped by the imposition on Poland, as an integral part of the peace settlement in 1919, of the Minorities' Treaty, which the powerful Jewish lobby at the Paris conference had insisted upon.[19] The Poles, however, took offence at what they regarded as an infringement of the state's sovereignty and an insult to Poland's long and well-established tradition of tolerance of minority groups. It might have been far more useful for the Allied statesmen to have decided upon Poland's borders. As it was, while her western border with Germany was delineated, except for Upper Silesia, her other borders remained fluid and caused Poland to become embroiled in a series of wars with her neighbours, including Soviet Russia, the Ukrainians and the Lithuanians.[20] In 1918/19 Poland was therefore a state without a definitive and internationally recognized territorial status. Complicating the attempt to solve this crucial matter was Poland's lack of the basic infrastructure of a state, which had to be built afresh from the fissiparous remnants of the former partitionist powers. A uniform civil service, judiciary, police, educational system and, not least, a unified army needed to be developed without delay in order to provide a coherent and workable state authority.

Political and governmenal stability would seem to have been absolutely necessary before any of these problems could be addressed with realistic expectations of success. But the Poland of the early post-war era also lacked that basic ingredient, which may be partly explained by the paucity of the political legacy of Partition. Service in the prewar *Duma* or *Reichstag* by a handful of Polish politicians hardly provided adequate training or experience for running the Polish state and, of course, none of them had an understanding of the parliamentary democratic system which, for effective operation, demanded a spirit of compromise, particularly at a time when the country was under so much pressure on many fronts.[21] The electorate was also politically immature and fragmented.

The individualism for which the Poles had been notorious throughout Europe since the eighteenth century, when their country was known as 'the Republic of Anarchy', was still too much in evidence for Poland's own good. Consequently, Polish political life was soon characterized by extreme volatility and factionalism, with no fewer than 92 officially registered parties representing not only the principal traditions of Nationalism, Socialism and Populism, but different shades of these, as well as the ethnic minority constituencies. Until 1926 the National Democrats (*Endecja*) were the most influential single party, but also prominent were the Polish Socialist Party (PPS) and the three peasant parties, which united in 1931.[22] As a result of the first fully fledged national elections, in November 1922, seventeen parties won seats in parliament (*Sejm*). Cabinets were composed of shaky and transient coalitions: between 1918 and 1926 there were fourteen of them, a record even more dubious than that of the Weimar Republic. Furthermore, in the immediate aftermath of the right-wing assassination in December 1922 of the country's first President, Gabriel Narutowicz, a civil war was narrowly averted by the tough intervention of a new government led by General Władysław Sikorski, a hero of the Polish–Soviet War.

Remarkably, however, developments in these early years relating to the imperatives of integration and reconstruction at home and the achievement of viability an independent state in the international sphere were not unduly hindered by the absence of political harmony. It was undeniable that Poland was having to start from scratch, with few material resources and few friends, a situation which in most other countries would quickly have brought catastrophe. Many contemporaries did indeed write off Poland as a hopeless case. Yet it was not fully appreciated that amidst their seemingly irrevocable adversity, the Poles had the intrinsic ability to invoke a number of less tangible but no less significant elements in their favour. These constituted the unquenchable 'Polish Spirit'.

In the first instance, the Poles, of whatever social or political background, were animated by an intense national pride and patriotism which, having been nurtured during the interminable years of foreign oppression, was ready in 1918 to explode into a creative energy on behalf of the national cause.[23] Second, they had an expansive capacity for improvisation, which often allowed them to defy the logical odds against them in a variety of predicaments. Third, the powerful religious commitment of the vast majority of ethnic Poles, a vital part of their sense of national identity, was carried over from the partitionist era into the new Polish state. The Catholic Church had been the mainstay of 'Polishness' in the nineteenth century, and effortlessly coalesced with patriotism to emerge as a major social and moral influence after 1918.[24] The Polish–Vatican Concordat of 1925 formalized its leading role and status. In addition, the preserved 'Polishness' that encompassed a sophisticated cultural heritage and civilization which, traditionally, had been oriented towards the West, provided a secure platform for the country's successful development in the new age of independence. Finally, the nation shared a pride in the virtues of Polish arms, a tradition which in modern times took its inspiration from the victory of King Jan Sobieski over the Turks at the Battle of Vienna in 1683, continued in the insurrections of the nineteenth century and, more recently, was animated by the exploits of the Polish Legions and other units in the First World War. This was not a militarism of the nefarious type that evolved in Prussia (and, later, Germany), but rather a belief in the Polish Armed Forces as the ultimate defender of the honour and integrity of the nation, personified by Józef Piłsudski.[25] With these self-made advantages, it is perhaps not too surprising, after all, that within a short time Poland was able to confound her numerous critics and adversaries by recording impressive achievements in many principal areas of national life.

In a series of enforced wars against her neighbours, Poland finally established her borders on mainly favourable terms. Lwów and Eastern Galicia were secured from the Ukrainians by July 1919, large parts of Upper Silesia as a result of three Polish Risings against the Germans and an Allied-supervised plebiscite in 1921,[26] Wilno from the Lithuanians and, most important of all, the eastern provinces following the war against the Soviet Bolsheviks in 1919–20 and the Treaty of Riga in March 1921. These resounding triumphs of the Polish Army were only partially offset by the diplomatic failure to bring Cieszyn under Polish jurisdiction: this bone of contention with Czechoslovakia, which had broken an earlier agreement with the Poles over the area, was finally settled satisfactorily in 1938.

By the early 1920s, also, the institutional framework of the state was in place, thus providing the basis for progress in other important spheres. The economy, further weakened by heavy military expenditure, fell into a downward cycle which culminated in Autumn 1923 in a hyperinflation comparable with that of Weimar Germany. However, again following the German pattern, a series of bold financial reforms in 1924 during the premiership of Władysław Grabski set the country on the road to recovery and growth. A new uniform currency, the *zloty*, was successfully introduced, and was complemented by the setting up of the Bank of Poland as the centrepiece of the banking and financial sectors. A revamped fiscal system made possible the more efficient collection of taxes, thus allowing the national budget to be balanced for the first time in 1926 and continue to be so until 1930/31. Indeed, in the late 1920s a budget surplus was recorded. A 'stabilization loan' from American bankers in 1927 completed the overhaul of the monetary system.[27]

With government encouragement, investment in industry rose, albeit modestly, and by 1928 unemployment had all but disappeared. But for the Tariff War with Germany beginning in 1925 and lasting until 1934, Poland's economic revival would have been even more striking. As it was, the standard of living for most improved, with real wages increasing in some skilled occupations by up to 40 per cent. In 1924 work began on the construction of Gdynia as Poland's major port on the Baltic, a development of considerable national pride, particularly as Danzig was eclipsed before long in terms of volume of commercial traffic. The General Strike in Britain in 1926 allowed Polish coal exports to fill the resultant gap in European markets. An ambitious programme of public utility construction, mainly of roads and bridges, was also successfully launched. Altogether, the general resurgence of the European economy from the mid-1920s was undoubtedly a factor not to be underestimated, but Poland's advances owed more still to her own endeavours and determination to overcome problems.

The public social welfare sector was not neglected amidst this feverish activity. The progressive social reforms of 1918–19 could now be more fully implemented. With an avowed commitment to maintaining the integrity of the family, reflecting the unofficial but palpable Catholic ethos of the state, insurance provision was made for health, accident, unemployment and old age. Juvenile and female labour was given protective legislation, and farm labourers, who made up about 15 per cent of the rural population, were awarded obligatory collective labour contracts. Furthermore, the principle of the eight-hour day became more widely observed, as did statutory arbitration procedures.[28] Poland's public welfare, therefore, compared favourably with that of more industrialized countries in Europe, including Britain and France, and was not far behind that of Germany.

The educational system was soon changed beyond recognition, reflecting the high priority traditionally allotted to this area by the Poles when given the opportunity. After all, prior to the Partitions, Poland's universities had been among the most renowned in Europe. That pre-eminence was steadily being reaffirmed by the late 1920s, as Polish mathematicians from the University in

Lwów, chemists, physicists, philosophers, linguists, anthropologists and many others brought international recognition and distinction to Polish scholarship. A new Catholic University at Lublin was founded at the beginning of the period, and by the mid-1930s Poland's universities, though not free of the growing influence of radical politics, were providing a stimulating atmosphere for some 48,000 students, an increasing number of whom came from a working-class or peasant background.[29] The Polish intelligentsia thus expanded in numbers and self-confidence despite the rigours of the Depression.

Further down the educational scale, a compulsory and free primary school system was set up in 1919 and thousands of new schools were built, as well as teacher-training and technical colleges, so that within a decade a notable decrease in illiteracy levels, which had been especially high among the young Ukrainian and Byelorussian communities, was achieved. A major reform of the schools system in 1932 brought more improvements. Culture of the popular and the more formal type also flourished, often in spectacular fashion, and the world of literature, music and theatre produced a dazzling array of talented personalities, many of whom were esteemed as much abroad as at home.[30] The milieu of polonized Jewry was particularly prominent in these spheres.[31]

The 1920s did not witness any real advances, however, as far as the assimilation of the national minorities was concerned, despite the considerable freedoms which they enjoyed from the state for their own organizational activity in politics, religion, education and culture. They also enjoyed further protection under the Constitution of March 1921. The Germans, Ukrainians and Jews in particular continued to nurse a range of grievances which the state tried to address within a framework of limited resources. The policy of 'polonization' favoured by the Right could not be implemented to any great extent because of the ongoing political turmoil, so that at best an uneasy stalemate ensued.[32]

A decisive turning-point in the history of the Second Republic came in May 1926, when Marshal Piłsudski effected his controversial *coup d'état*.[33] It was prompted by his growing fear that the unstable and often tumultuous parliamentary system, with its endemic graft and corruption, was putting Poland's independence in serious jeopardy, particularly as he felt that the effectiveness of his beloved Army was being compromised by a group of squabbling politicians. Piłsudski was a staunch opponent of the nationalist Right (*Endecja*) which had been heavily involved in government from 1918, and believed that the time had come for him, a self-styled 'man of destiny', to take over and steer Poland out of crisis.[34] The depth of that crisis had been underlined for him by the faltering economic reforms of the Grabski government and, more seriously perhaps, by the implications of the Locarno Pact of 1925, whereby Germany had recognized and accepted her western but not her eastern borders. The Marshal was as much perturbed by the threat of German as of Soviet revanchism towards Poland.

The coup was supported by the parties of the Left, including the outlawed Communist Party of Poland (KPP), who saw it as thwarting the threat of fascism; but for the *Endecja* and its centrist allies the coup was an outrageous provocation. None the less, it is undeniable that the Marshal's *Sanacja* regime brought a measure of stability to political life, even if the price was the progressive emasculation of parliament and a corresponding increase in authoritarianism of a populist kind. Piłsudski was never to be a dictator in the mould of a Hitler, Mussolini or Stalin, but he did bring strength and a sense of purposeful direction to his aim of defending the national interest as he understood it.[35] He attracted as many committed admirers as he did inveterate critics in Poland, whereas international opinion regarded him with admiration and respect, indeed as personifying Poland.[36] At the same time, although he tried to rally broad support in the country, for example through the Non-Party Bloc for Cooperation with the Government (BBWR), he was not averse to employing other, less desirable tactics to maintain his regime. A certain amount of electoral manipulation and intimidation of political opponents was brought to bear, notoriously when some of the most vociferous of the Communist, Ukrainian and radical Right protagonists were placed in the Bereza Kartuska internment camp in 1934. Though defended on the grounds of national security, such actions tarnished the image of Poland abroad.

The onset of the Depression, which hit Poland with crushing severity, ensured that the second decade of independence would present additional challenges to which there were unlikely to be easy answers. In this respect, however, Poland was no different from any other major European country. The Depression brought unprecedented levels of unemployment, a slump in business and commerce, falling prices for agricultural products and plummeting living standards, especially among the peasantry in the countryside, where accelerating population growth, lack of investment in machinery and continuation of outdated farming methods was compounded by piecemeal agrarian reform.[37] Land Reform Acts in July 1920 and December 1925 had been stifled by political opposition from the powerful aristocratic lobby and by government inertia. The amount of land redistributed from the large estates to the peasantry was relatively modest, though it should also be said that that was by no means the answer to the agrarian problem.[38] Widespread poverty, ignorance and resentment amounted to a lethal cocktail in the countryside, encouraging political radicalism and violent strikes, especially in 1936–7, when many deaths resulted from clashes with police.

The political situation was further radicalized from several other directions. The Depression era saw a noticeable increase in ethnic tension. Elements of the Ukrainian opposition took to terrorism, which included the assassination of prominent Polish officials, thus inviting several 'pacification' exercises by the government in Eastern Galicia. The German minority's disaffection increased, while anti-Semitism and Jewish polonophobia contributed to a climate of fear and anxiety.[39] The government's steadfast adherence to a deflationary strategy as its way of coping with the economic crisis, though successful in preserving the value of the currency, meant that there was no alleviation of the appalling social consequences, which included the virtual disintegration of the public welfare system because of chronic underfunding. The unexpected and much-lamented early death of Piłsudski from cancer in May 1935 epitomized for many Poles the tragedy of these years. It seemed as if all their efforts to make Poland strong had been in vain. Strangely, however, it transpired that the Marshal's death marked another important turning-point, which brought renewed hope and progress on many fronts.

There were clear indications that by 1935/36 the worst of the economic crisis was over and that Poland could resume the development that had been so vigorously interrupted by the Depression and its far-reaching reverberations. The introduction by the government of a four-year investment programme, the centrepiece of which was the Central Industrial Area in the Warsaw-Kraków-Lwów triangle, was a significant step in state intervention in the economy. The relative scarcity of private capital made etatism unavoidable, and besides, this allowed government to combine its industrial strategy with its military needs, particularly at a time of rising international tension caused by Hitler's expansionist foreign policy and Stalin's mischief-making.[40]

Within two years industrial output had exceeded the levels of 1928, exports of coal, steel, textiles and crude oil were booming, a new chemical industry was established in the south-east, and agricultural prices began to recover. A budget surplus was once again recorded in 1938, the national debt fell by one third and the national income rose by 20 per cent by the same year. Living standards began to improve for all groups, except the poorest in the countryside, and unemployment fell substantially. The capital, Warsaw, epitomized this revival by re-emerging as one of Europe's most attractive and interesting capitals. Its Royal Castle fully restored in all its former glory and a National Museum built, Warsaw was again a favourite posting for diplomats.[41] Poles began to exude new confidence. The good manners, civility and public decency that had been a salient feature of Polish life in the late 1920s reappeared, as did a feeling for quality and style.

The post-Piłsudski *Sanacja* regime was characterized by an increasing approximation to authoritarianism on the basis of the new Constitution of April 1935, and to militant nationalism under the influence, paradoxically, of the ideology of the *Endecja*. This was intimated, for instance, by the ultra-nationalist, conservative and Catholic ideology of the government-sponsored organization, Camp of National Unity (OZON), which was set up in 1937.[42] Relations between the state and the ethnic minorities, especially the Jews, consequently deteriorated, though their stubborn refusal to put a realistic perspective on their problems and to reach a *rapprochment* with the state was as much to blame for the impasse.

The future wartime experiences of all these minorities made their position in the Second Republic before 1939 appear very favourable. In the meantime, as the international atmosphere became more ominous, ethnic Poles experienced a growing sense of patriotic unity which they had not had since the earliest days of independence. Constructive cooperation and solidarity among the parties replaced confrontation and recrimination to a considerable degree, as shown by national elections in November 1938, which produced a broad consensus in favour of the government.[43] Patriotic loyalty to Poland transcended many previous differences and divisions in the face of the common enemy.

In the space of a mere 20 years of independence the Second Republic had made quite remarkable progress in many important spheres, when its severe disadvantages and obstacles at home and abroad are taken fully into account. The cultural and educational spheres were unequivocal successes, and no less important was the consolidation of the Republic's territory in the early 1920s by the victorious efforts of the Polish Army. Its victory over the Soviet Bolsheviks at Warsaw in August 1920 was crucial to Poland's survival as an independent state, and to the well-being of Europe as a whole.

Significant problems remained to be solved, of course, in some other areas. Too many capital and labour resources continued to be invested in the backward agricultural sector, and industrialization was still comparatively underdeveloped, though the indications in the late 1930s were that, given peaceable conditions, the economy as a whole was prepared for longer-term growth. One expert observer has gone as far as to affirm that Poland's economic development before 1939 was 'outstanding'.[44] Material living standards were perhaps not yet as high as those in the advanced industrial countries, such as Germany, Britain or France, but the gap was being closed and, in any case, in other non-material, qualitative terms, Poland was at least the equal of all of them. For example, it was a society that did not suffer from high crime rates, drugs, divorce or abortion, and the incidence of pornography, white slavery and prostitution was far lower than in Western countries. On the other hand, the relationship of the national minorities to the state was still a matter of acute concern.

In general, however, Poland exhibited a sense of purpose, vitality and creativity that boded well for the future. On the eve of the Second World War, she had asserted her viability as a free, sovereign, proud and increasingly successful state at the centre of European affairs, an achievement that was all the more praiseworthy because it had come about through her own, unassisted efforts. The deep pride which Poles felt in their country explains why, from 1939 until 1945, they fought courageously on battlefields all over Europe at the side of the Allies to restore it to that pre-eminent status.[45]

NOTES

1. The best general survey is P. S. Wandycz, *The Lands of Partitioned Poland, 1795–1918* (University of Washington Press, Seattle, 1974), but also useful for background are S. J. Blejwas, *Realism in Polish Politics: Warsaw Positivism and National Survival in Nineteenth Century Poland* (Yale University Press, New Haven, 1984), and A. Bromke, *Poland's Politics: Idealism versus Realism* (Harvard University Press, Cambridge, Mass., 1967).
2. Detailed information in T. Komarnicki, *The Rebirth of the Polish Republic: A Study in the Diplomatic History of Europe, 1914–1920* (Heinemann, London, 1957); L. L. Gerson, *Woodrow Wilson and the Rebirth of Poland, 1914–1920* (Yale University Press, New Haven, 1953); K. Lundgreen-Nielson, *The Polish Problem at the Paris Peace Conference: A Study of the Policies of the Great Powers and the Poles, 1918–1919* (Odense University Press, Odense, 1979); W. Sukiennicki, *East-Central Europe during World War I: From Foreign Domination to National Independence* (Boulder, Co., 1984, 2 volumes); and the massive work by J. Pajewski, *Pierwsza wojna światowa 1914–1918* (PWN, Warsaw, 1991).
3. N. Davies, *God's Playground. A History of Poland. Volume II: 1795 to the Present* (Clarendon Press, Oxford, 1981), p. 392.
4. P. D. Stachura, 'The Second Polish Republic: An Historiographical Outline', in Peter D. Stachura (ed.), *Poland Between the Wars, 1918–1939* (Macmillan, London, 1998. Something of the broader picture is conveyed in J. Tomicki (ed.), *Polska Odrodzona 1918–1939* (PWN, Warsaw, 1982); H. Zieliński, *Historia Polski 1914–1939* (Wrocław, 1983); and by a former French ambassador to Poland, L. Noël, *La Pologne entre deux mondes* (La Sorbonne, Paris, 1984).
5. Davies, *God's Playground*, II, p. 434.

6. The view of A. Polonsky in R. F. Leslie (ed.), *The History of Poland since 1863* (Cambridge University Press, 1983), pp. 206–7.
7. N. Davies, *Heart of Europe: A Short History of Poland* (Clarendon Press, Oxford, 1984), p. 467, where he harshly describes Jędrzej Giertych, author of *In Defence of My Country* (privately published, London, 1980), as a 'nationalist polemicist'.
8. Z. Landau and J. Tomaszewski, *The Polish Economy in the Twentieth Century* (Routledge, London, 1985), pp. 27 ff., 115–16. More statistical data in J. Jankowski and A. Serafiński, *Polska w Liczbach* (Polish Army Education Bureau, London, 1941).
9. H. Feindt (ed.), *Studien zur Kulturgeschichte des deutschen Polenbildes, 1848–1939* (Harrassowitz, Wiesbaden, 1995), provides an outline, which may be supplemented by K. Fiedor, J. Sobczak and W. Wrzesiński, 'The Image of the Poles in Germany and of the Germans in Poland in the Interwar Years and Its Role in Shaping the Relations Between the Two States', *Polish Western Affairs*, 19 (1978), No. 2, pp. 203–28.
10. F. L. Carsten, *The Reichswehr and Politics, 1918–1933* (Oxford University Press, 1966), pp. 140–41. See also R. Schattkowsky, *Deutschland und Polen von 1918–19 bis 1925* (Peter Lang, Frankfurt/Main, 1994); P. Madajczyk, *Polityka i koncepcje polityczne Gustawa Stresemana wobec Polski (1915–1929)* (INP, Warsaw, 1991); C. Fink, A. Frohn, J. Heideking (eds), *Genoa, Rapallo, and European Reconstruction in 1922* (Cambridge University Press, 1991).
11. Good coverage, for example, in A. Korczyński and S. Świetochowski (eds), *Poland Between Germany and Russia, 1926–1939* (New York, 1975); J. Korbel, *Poland Between East and West: Soviet and German Diplomacy Towards Poland 1919–1933* (Princeton University Press, Princeton, NJ, 1963); P. S. Wandycz, *Soviet–Polish Relations, 1917–1921* (Harvard University Press, Cambridge, Mass., 1969); A. M. Cienciala and T. Komarnicki, *From Versailles to Locarno: Keys to Polish Foreign Policy, 1919–1925* (University Press of Kansas, Lawrence, 1984).
12. Poland concluded full alliances with France and Romania in 1921. France, however, grew more and more lukewarm, partly because the economic and political problems of the Third Republic weakened its diplomatic influence in European affairs. A recent monograph throws some new light on the subject: A. Essen, *Polska a Mała Ententa, 1920–1934* (PWN, Warsaw, 1992), especially chs. 3–5.
13. Details in P. Latawski (ed.), *The Reconstruction of Poland, 1914–1923* (Macmillan, London, 1992); F. Zweig, *Poland Between Two Wars: A Critical Study of Social and Economic Changes* (Secker & Warburg, London, 1944); W. Roszkowski, *Landowners in Poland, 1918–1939* (Cambridge University Press, 1991).
14. P. D. Stachura, 'National Identity and the Ethnic Minorities in Early Postwar Poland', in Stachura (ed.), *Poland Between the Wars*; J. Tomaszewski, *Ojczyzna nie tylko Polaków. Mniejszości narodowe*

    w Polsce w latach 1918–1939 (Warsaw, 1985); S. Horak, *Poland and Her National Minorities, 1919–39* (Vantage Press, New York, 1961).

15. From an extensive literature, R. Blanke, *Orphans of Versailles: The Germans in Western Poland, 1918–1939* (University Press of Kentucky, Lexington, 1993); T. Urban, *Deutsche in Polen* (Beck, Munich, 1993); T. Hunczak (ed.), *Ukraine and Poland in Documents, 1918–1922* (Shevchenko Scientific Society, New York, 1983); S. Skrzypek, *The Problem of Eastern Galicia* (Polish Association for the South-Eastern Provinces, London, 1948); A. Żółtowski, *Border of Europe: A Study of the Polish Eastern Provinces* (Hollis & Carter, London, 1950); E. Koko, *Wolni z wolnymi, PPS wobec kwestii ukraińskiej w latach 1918–1925* (Gdańsk University, Gdańsk, 1991).

16. See C. Abramsky, M. Jachimczyk and A. Polonsky (eds), *The Jews in Poland* (Blackwell, Oxford, 1986); Y. Gutman, E. Mendelsohn, J. Reinharz and C. Shmeruk (eds), *The Jews of Poland Between Two World Wars* (University Press of New England, Hanover, 1989); J. Marcus, *Social and Political History of the Jews in Poland, 1919–1939* (Mouton, New York, 1983).

17. A review in I. Lewin and N. M. Gelber, *A History of Polish Jewry during the Renewal of Poland* (Shengold Publishers, New York, 1990).

18. P. D. Stachura, 'The Battle of Warsaw, August 1920, and the Development of the Second Polish Republic', in Stachura (ed.), *Poland between the Wars*; see further J. A. Drobnicki, 'The Russo–Polish War, 1919–1920: A Bibliography of Materials in English', *The Polish Review*, 42 (1997), No. 1, pp. 95–104, and J. Piłsudski, *Year 1920* (Piłsudski Institute, New York, 1972).

19. M. Levene, *War, Jews and the New Europe: The Diplomacy of Lucien Wolf, 1914–1919* (Oxford University Press, 1992); *idem*, 'Britain, a British Jew, and Jewish Relations with the New Poland: The Making of the Polish Minorities Treaty of 1919', *Polin*, 8 (1994), pp. 14-41.

20. Informative analysis in M. Wrzosek, *Wojny o granice Polski Odrodzonej 1918–1921* (BWH, Warsaw, 1992).

21. The theme is discussed in E. Chmielewski, *The Polish Question in the Russian State Duma* (University of Tennessee Press, Knoxville, 1970).

22. Detailed coverage in A. Ajnenkiel, *Od 'rządow ludowych' do przewrotu majowego. Zarys dziejów politycznych Polski 1918–1926* (Warsaw, 1979); A Polonsky, *Politics in Independent Poland, 1921–1939: The Crisis of Constitutional Government* (Oxford University Press, 1972); Leslie (ed.), *History of Poland*, pp. 125–207; R. M. Watt, *Bitter Glory: Poland and Its Fate. 1918 to 1939* (Simon & Schuster, New York, 1979), pp. 190 ff., R. Wapiński, *Narodowa Demokracja 1893–1939* (Wrocław, 1980).

23. P. Brock, *Nationalism and Populism in Partitioned Poland* (Orbis, London, 1968), *passim.*

24. S. Gomułka and A. Polonsky (eds), *Polish Paradoxes* (Routledge, London, 1990), p. 12; wider discussion in B. Grott, *Nacjonalizm i Religia* (Kraków, 1984).

25. Davies, *God's Playground*, II, pp. 271, 404, 419.

26. The issue is viewed from two contrasting perspectives in T. Hunt Tooley, *National Identity and Weimar Germany: Upper Silesia and the Eastern Border. 1918–1922* (University of Nebraska Press, Lincoln, 1997), and P. Leśniewski, 'Three Insurrections: Upper Silesia, 1919–1921', in Stachura (ed.), *Poland Between the Wars*.

27. Landau and Tomaszewski, *Polish Economy*, pp. 73, 80.

28. *Ibid.*, p. 55; Zweig, *Poland Between Two Wars*, pp. 139–50.

29. It is estimated that in 1935 18 per cent of higher education students were from a peasant background and 4 per cent from the industrial working class: figures in J. Coutouvidis, A. Garlicki and J. Reynolds, 'Poland', in S. Salter and J. Stevenson (eds), *The Working Class and Politics in Europe and America, 1929–1945* (Longman, London, 1990), p. 174.

30. C. Miłosz, *A History of Polish Literature* (London, 1969); R. Dyboski, *Poland in World Civilization* (Barrett, New York, 1950), chs. 8 and 9.

31. J. Malinowski and A. Rodzińska, 'Jewish Artistic Circles in Interwar Poland', *Polish Art Studies*, 10 (1989), pp. 55–66; E. Prokopowna and M. Pilch, 'In Quest of Cultural Identity. Polish-Jewish Literature in the Interwar Period', *The Polish Review*, 32 (1987), No. 4, pp. 415–38.

32. Stachura, 'National Identity', *op. cit.*

33. J. Rothschild, *Pilsudski's Coup d'Etat* (Columbia University Press, New York, 1966), to be supplemented with A. Czubiński, *Przewrót majowy 1926 roku* (MAW, Warsaw, 1989).

34. The most recent biographies in English are W. Jędrzejewicz, *Pilsudski. A Life for Poland* (Hippocrene Books, New York, 1982), and, very critical, A. Garlicki, *Josef Pilsudski, 1867–1935* (Scholar Press, New York, 1995). A useful source is D. R. Gillie (ed.), *Joseph Pilsudski. The Memories of a Polish Revolutionary and Soldier* (Faber and Faber, London, 1931).

35. Overviews in A. Ajnenkiel, *Polska po przewrocie majowym. Zarys dziejów politycznych Polski 1926–1939* (Warsaw, 1980); *idem, Sejmy i konstytucja w Polsce 1918–1939* (Warsaw, 1968); A. Chojnowski, *Piłsudczycy u władzy. Dzieje Bezpartyjnego Bloku Wspolpracy z Rządem* (Warsaw, 1986); and J. Faryś, *Piłsudski i piłsudczycz. Z dziejów koncepcji polityczno-ustrojowej 1918–1939* (Szczecin, 1991).

36. For example, Z. J. Gąsiorowski, 'Joseph Pilsudski in the Light of British Reports', *Slavonic and East European Review*, 50 (1972), pp. 558–69.

37. O. A. Narkiewicz, *The Green Flag: Polish Populist Politics, 1867–1970* (Croom Helm, London, 1976), pp. 178 ff.

38. As argued by W. Roszkowski, 'Large Estates and Small Farms in the Polish Agrarian Economy between the Wars (1918–1939)', *Journal of European Economic History*, 16 (1987), No. 1, pp. 75–88.

39. E. D. Wynot, ' "A Necessary Cruelty": The Emergence of Official Anti-Semitism in Poland, 1936–1939', *American Historical Review*, 76 (1971), No. 4, pp. 1035–58.

40. Landau and Tomaszewski, *Polish Economy*, pp. 117–28, 131 ff.
41. E. D. Wynot, *Warsaw Between the World Wars: Profile of the Capital City in a Developing Land, 1918–1939* (Boulder, Co., 1983) provides a comprehensive picture.
42. In-depth analysis in E. D. Wynot, *Polish Politics in Transition: The Camp of National Unity and the Struggle for Power, 1935–1939* (University of Georgia Press, Athens, Georgia, 1974), and J. M. Majchrowski, *Silni, zwarci, gotowi. Myśl polityczna Obozu Zjednoczenia Narodowego* (Warsaw, 1985). The Soviet dimension is analysed by J. Pagel, *Polen und die Sowjetunion, 1938–1939* (Steiner, Wiesbaden, 1992).
43. Davies, *Heart of Europe*, pp. 127–47.
44. J. J. Taylor, *The Economic Development of Poland, 1919–1950* (Cornell University Press, Ithaca, New York, 1952), p. 153.
45. The generational angle on the achievements of the inter-war era is featured in R. Wapiński, *Pokolenia Drugiej Rzeczypospolitej* (Ossolineum, Warsaw, 1991). A useful overview is J. Garliński, *Poland in the Second World War* (Macmillan, London, 1985).

3 The Polish–Jewish Symbiosis in the Second Republic, 1918–39

Polish–Jewish relations during the first half of the twentieth century are invariably characterized in the most negative of terms. Many historians, and not only those who are Jewish or of Jewish origin, have excoriated the Second Polish Republic in particular for being vehemently or even uniquely anti-Semitic. They have also often argued that Poles bear a considerable measure of responsibility for the appalling tragedy of the Holocaust, the organized and systematic extermination of some six million Jews by the Third Reich during the Second World War.[1] The anti-Semitism attributed to inter-war Poland is interpreted as an essential preparation or dress rehearsal for the mass atrocities of wartime. In short, the Holocaust is depicted as the inevitable culmination of pre-war anti-Semitism, not simply in National Socialist Germany, which pursued an official policy of racist anti-Semitism, but also in Poland, which did not.[2]

The charge of Polish complicity in one of the greatest crimes of modern times could hardly be more grave, not least because it has undoubtedly helped to form attitudes about Poland and Poles in the wider world down to the present day. Poland has been portrayed as an accomplice of a thoroughly discredited and universally reviled Hitlerian regime, with all the unfortunate consequences that this entails. The charge attaches a certain stigma to a country which, otherwise, has itself experienced profound and lasting suffering and misfortune this century at the hands of friend and foe alike, including, of course, the Nazis. Any evaluation of this important matter demands the establishment of an appropriate historical context, which logically means beginning with an assessment of the nature, extent and significance of relations between the Second Republic and its extensive Jewish community before 1939.

The first national census of 1921 recorded a total Jewish population in Poland of 2.85 million, which by 1939 had risen to about 3.5 million, or approximately 10 per cent of the whole.[3] The figure would have been higher still if 395,000 Jews had not emigrated during the inter-war period. The Jews were conspicuous not only on account of their considerable numbers. An overwhelmingly urban group in a predominantly rural and agrarian country, they constituted a large percentage of the population of most of Poland's major cities, Warsaw, Kraków, Lwów, Łódź and Wilno,[4] and in the small townships (*Shtetlekh*) of Eastern Poland they were frequently in a clear majority. While a relatively small number of Jews, about 8 or 9 per cent, were assimilated, in that they spoke Polish and considered themselves to be at least mainly Polish in sentiment, loyalty, attitude and social convention,[5] the vast majority were distinguished by their physical, emotional and spiritual detachment from the ethnic Polish population.[6] They spoke Yiddish or, much less often, Hebrew, wore distinctive clothing, and were concentrated in particular areas of economic life – in artisan trades such as printing, shoemaking and garment manufacture. The Jews dominated the small entrepreneurial and commercial class throughout the period, and were also heavily represented in banking, financial services, insurance and the liberal professions, especially medicine, publishing and law. Their social and economic exclusivity was also reflected in and underpinned by their equally diversified political activity: alongside the conservative and assimilationist Orthodox Jews of the *Agudath Yisrael*, representing mainly upper and middle-class propertied, comfortably off and educated Jews, were parties of the Jewish lower middle class and proletarian masses, the pro-Marxist *Bund* (General Jewish Workers' Union), the Zionists (of different type), the Folkists and smaller socialist groups.[7]

This substantial Jewish population was clearly not homogeneous in any major sense. They were divided, often acrimoniously, from a social, economic, financial, religious, educational and political perspective. Collectively, however, the Jewish minority shared two important unifying characteristics: firstly, they were, in general, materially better-off than their Polish neighbours, with incomes during the periods of relative prosperity in the late 1920s and late 1930s of up to 40 per cent higher; secondly, they opposed the establishment of an independent Polish state in 1918–19, and continued this hostility, in varying degrees, thereafter. This raises the barely mentioned theme of polonophobia, alongside the persistent, heavily emphasized theme of anti-Semitism.

Both Jewish anti-Polonism and Polish anti-Semitism predated the advent of the Second Republic. These regrettable phenomena had grown markedly during the second half of the nineteenth century, following the failure of the 1863 Uprising against the Russians.[8] Polish and Jewish interests then began to diverge more sharply than ever before, not least over the question of how Poland was to regain her independence from the powers who had partitioned her at the end of the previous century. Against a backdrop of tensions arising from a degree of industrial and commercial expansion, in which Jews played a conspicuous role, emerging nationalism on both sides (National Democracy and Zionism), eventual disillusionment with the limited benefits of 'Organic Work' and the spread of national and class consciousness to the peasantry and divisive partitionist policies, Polish–Jewish relations were already seriously deteriorating before the outbreak of the First World War. Too many Poles and too many Jews came to regard the other as different and alien.[9] The Polish view was that the Jews had also become defenders of the partitionist status quo and hence were opposed to the cause of Polish independence, which was being advanced above all by the National Democratic Party under Roman Dmowski and the Polish Socialist Party (Revolutionary Faction) led by Józef Piłsudski.

As a consequence of manipulative policies by Germany, Russia and Austria-Hungary, coinciding with renewed efforts by the Poles to exploit the volatile circumstances of war to further their own agenda for independence, relations with the Jews frequently worsened still further. By the time President Woodrow Wilson of the United States presented his famous Fourteen Points as the Western Allies' programme for a post-war peace settlement, which included the re-establishment of an independent Poland, powerful Jewish forces in America, Britain and France as well as in Poland itself were preparing to offer vigorous opposition to that specific objective.[10]

The busy, well-connected Jewish lobby at the Paris Peace Conference in 1919 ultimately failed to prevent the creation of an independent Polish state in the wake of the collapse of the former partitioning powers, or to have the Jews officially recognized as a national autonomous element in the new state. It did succeed, however, in having incorporated into the settlement for Poland the Minorities' Treaty, whose purpose was to provide legal and constitutional protection for the sizeable Ukrainian, Byelorussian, German and, especially, Jewish minorities who formed about one-third of the citizenry of the Second Republic.[11] Many Poles, affronted by what they regarded as an unjustified encroachment on their sovereignty and lack of trust in their tradition of tolerance, had their worst fears of the Jews apparently confirmed at a most poignant moment in their modern history. The Jews were unquestionably, it seemed, the enemy within, a view further strengthened by the vociferous campaign of anti-Polish denunciation in the world's press that was conducted by various Jewish organizations and spokesmen during these early years of Polish independence. In short, at the very moment of Poland's rebirth anti-Semitism and anti-Polonism were much in evidence, each perniciously reinforcing the other.

It cannot be said that the relationship quickly improved. On the contrary, in a situation where the Polish state strove to consolidate its freedom and independence amidst the most unpropitious economic and political conditions, hostility between Poles and Jews was heightened. Poland's need to reconstruct her economy and infrastructure from what little had been left viable from the depredations of partition and war, and her need to establish and secure her frontiers in a series of wars from 1918 to 1921, only served to aggravate an already tense and unfruitful situation with the Jews. The crucial event which starkly exposed the depth and extent of the difficulty was the Polish–Soviet War of 1919–20, when a substantial portion of the Jewish minority, especially in Eastern Poland, evinced unequivocal sympathy and support for the invading Red Army.[12] Some Jews did fight and die for Poland in this conflict, but they were unrepresentative of their community as a whole. An understandably distrustful Polish government, acting in the interests of national security, was compelled to intern certain numbers of Jews in the military internment camp at Jabłonna for the duration of the war. But at the same time, and illustrating the complexity and unpredictability which often informed Polish–Jewish relations, around 600,000 Jewish refugees from the civil war in Russia were allowed to remain in Poland by 1921, and after his *coup d'état* in 1926 Marshal Piłsudski granted them Polish citizenship.[13]

The momentous victory of the Polish Army under Piłsudski's leadership at the decisive Battle of Warsaw in mid-August 1920, and the subsequent rout of the Bolsheviks on the Niemen and at Zamość,[14] could not obscure a dark and ominous chapter in Polish–Jewish relations. Moreover, it may be argued that the distrust, antagonism, even hatred displayed between sections of the two sides during the earliest years of Poland's independence were never fully overcome, exerting therefore a lasting negative influence right up to the outbreak of the Second World War. On the other hand, although both sides had legitimate complaints against the other, it is arguable that neither anti-Semitism nor polonophobia assumed the proportions or the consistency that has usually been suggested.

Until Piłsudski's coup in May 1926, the nationalist Centre-Right coalition governments which were invariably in power did not make any noticeable headway in improving Polish–Jewish relations, despite the well-meant but transient agreement (*Ugoda*) of July 1925 covering a wide range of issues of mutual concern.[15] It was undermined before long by growing doubts about its value in government circles, but mainly by the opposition to it from intransigent Zionists within the broad Jewish camp. In fact, given the influence in government and the public at large of the right-wing and overtly anti-Semitic National Democrats – the *Endecja* – and of the anti-Polish belligerence of Jewish leaders such as Yitshak Gruenbaum, it is perhaps not surprising that relations remained generally unfriendly. The *Endecja* had declared, after all, that the Jews, as an alien group, could not be assimilated into Polish society, while Gruenbaum, for example, had not only provocatively organized the Bloc of National Minorities to contest elections in 1922, but had also taken every opportunity within his declared policy of principled opposition to the government – any

Polish government – to voice his thunderous disapproval of just about everything undertaken by it. Gruenbaum may not have spoken for all Jews, but such was his wide influence and high profile that that particular nuance was lost on many Poles.[16]

Even so, the Jews were allowed to enjoy considerable freedoms to set up their own press, which published in Polish, Yiddish and Hebrew, build their own schools, hospitals, synagogues, cemeteries and orphanages, organize their own charities and trade unions, develop their own culture, religion, scholarship (YIVO in Wilno from 1925) and political parties, and to play a leading role in the economy, especially in textiles, food processing, shoemaking, clothing manufacture, sugar-refining, banking, insurance and other financial services, as well as several liberal professions. In consequence the Sunday Rest Law of November 1919, an important social reform applauded by the Polish Left but bitterly criticized by the Jews, was never fully implemented[17] and was therefore not an impediment to their rising levels of prosperity. They made up almost a quarter of university students, thus more than double their percentage in the population: in 1929, 40 per cent of university graduates were Jewish. The per capita income of Jews before the Depression was 30 to 40 per cent higher than the average for Poles. Jews, for instance, owned almost half of Warsaw's residential property until 1939.[18] These and other undisputed facts contradict claims of widespread discrimination and persecution of the Jews in the 1920s. In reality, a vibrant Jewish civilization flourished.[19]

Piłsudski's coup was warmly welcomed by an overwhelming majority of Jews as an opportunity to keep the Right at bay and to inaugurate a new era of partnership with the Poles. The Marshal was regarded by many as being to some degree philosemitic, not least because he had cooperated with Jews in the Polish Socialist Party (PPS) before 1914 and because it was appreciated that he was a staunch opponent of the chauvinism of the *Endecja*.[20] Before long, allegations surfaced of extensive Jewish influence in his ruling circle, with President Ignacy Mościcki and Prime Minister Kazimierz Bartel being singled out for their undisguised philosemitism. Concessions were quickly made by the new regime (*Sanacja*) to the Jews as part of an overall government initiative after 1926 to improve relations with all of Poland's principal minorities that included the reactivation in 1927 of the Institute for Research into Minority Questions in Warsaw.[21] In October 1927 the government reformed the Jewish communal organizations (*kehillah*), which pleased Orthodox Jewry most of all, and followed up by legalizing and accrediting the Orthodox religious schools (*cheder*). Assistance was also given to revive Jewish trade, and the economic upturn of the late 1920s brought many material benefits to them. Furthermore, the *numerus clausus* which sought to restrict Jewish entry to universities and other centres of higher education was banned.[22] Finally, in March 1931, legal restrictions on the civil rights of Jews that had been imposed in Tsarist times were abolished by governmental decree. None the less, many Jews were disappointed with the *Sanacja* regime for not doing more to improve their status and situation, although they at least took comfort from Piłsudski's strong grip on government. In a gesture of broad solidarity with it, the conservative *Agudath Yisrael* joined the Non-Party Bloc for Cooperation with the Government (BBWR) after its creation in January 1928.

The Depression, which was particularly severe and protracted in Poland, partly because of the government's inflexible deflationary strategy which was designed to preserve the stability of the currency (*złoty*), exercised a profoundly disruptive effect on society at large.[23] Rising unemployment, bankruptcies, business failures, falling wages and deepening poverty all combined to trigger social unrest, especially among the peasantry in a still largely unreformed and overpopulated countryside. The impoverishment of large sections of society naturally encompassed the Jews, but there is no compelling evidence that they were worse off than Poles, even after making allowance for their ineligibility, in many cases, for state unemployment benefit,[24] lack of state subsidies for their businesses, their large share of taxation[25] and falling prices for artisanal goods. Jewish relief agencies from abroad, particularly the United States, were allowed to provide help unhindered.[26]

The years of economic crisis from 1930 until 1935/36 probably threw into sharper relief than before the restrictions and disadvantages that the Jews did undoubtedly suffer, such as their exiguous employment in the civil service, the Army (except the legal branch and medical corps), state industry, the teaching profession and public transport.[27] On balance, the Jews, whose share of the total national income and national wealth remained until the war far in excess of their proportion of the population as a whole,[28] had a more solid material basis on which to survive the Depression than most Poles, who increasingly resented this state of affairs. It might also be noted that in a period when the government was adopting a tough stance against political opponents and subversives – a policy epitomized by the opening in July 1934 of the internment camp at Bereza Kartuska – no-one was sent there simply for being Jewish. Herman Lieberman, a Jew, was interned, but this was because of his oppositional activity as a leading member of the Polish Socialist Party.

The death of Marshal Piłsudski in May 1935 inaugurated a new, inauspicious chapter in Polish–Jewish relations, for with his hand no longer in place to restrain strong nationalist forces, including those within the *Sanacja* regime itself, the frustrations and resentments on both sides broke out into the open in a manner and with an intensity that had not been witnessed since the early 1920s. With the post-Piłsudski regime quickly moving to the Right to make common cause with many of the ideas of the *Endecja*, as demonstrated by the conservative, Catholic and nationalist programme (May 1938) – 'The 13 Theses of the OZN' – of the new, government-sponsored organization set up in 1937, the Camp of National Unity (*Obóz Zjednoczenia Narodowego*, OZN), anti-Semitism re-emerged as a salient feature of political and social life.[29] However, it assumed a mainly economic, religious and social rather than racial or political character, notwithstanding a degree of influence of Nazi Germany on the antics and outlook of the noisy but poorly supported extremists on the fascist radical Right, the National Radical Camp (ONR) and its offshoots, ONR-ABC and ONR-Falanga.[30]

The sporadic attacks on Jewish property, the boycotts of some Jewish businesses that appeared to be sanctioned by Prime Minister Felicjan Sławoj-Składkowski's infamous *'owszem'* speech before the *Sejm* on 4 June 1936, the partial restrictions on ritual slaughter (*Shechitah*) that were imposed in January 1937,[31] the introduction the same year of the *numerus clausus* and the 'ghetto bench' in universities,[32] the limits put on Jewish entry into some professions, the tougher implementation of the 1927 Guild Law which was disadvantageous to Jewish artisans, the Law on the Modernization of Bakeries and the extension of the state's control of industry (etatism) under an investment and development plan of 1936 for the new Central Industrial Area, all fell into the category of economic measures designed to rectify to some degree the imbalance created by the disproportionate influence exerted by the Jews in the economy as a whole, which was particularly noticeable at a time of acute difficulty. However, the economic revival that had become apparent in most sectors by 1937/8 helped to reduce anxieties, although the situation was not helped by the increase in international tension occasioned by Hitler's aggressive policies, some of which clearly posed a most serious threat to Poland and all Polish citizens.

The upsurge of anti-Semitism in the late 1930s in Poland was perhaps not helped by the attitude of the Catholic Church, most of whose hierarchy and clergy had been strong supporters of the *Endecja* from the beginning of the Republic's existence. Leading spokesmen, such as Cardinal Adam Sapieha of Kraków and the Primate, Cardinal August Hlond, issued public statements which underlined the Church's opposition to the conduct and attitudes of many Jews.[33] In his pastoral letter of 29 February 1936, Cardinal Hlond articulated the convictions of many Poles when he castigated Jews for promoting atheism, freemasonry and revolutionary Bolshevism (thus conjuring up the emotive notion of *Żydokomuna* or 'Jewish Bolshevism'), and for being heavily involved in objectionable activities that included usury, prostitution, white slavery and pornography. At the same time the Cardinal expressed his opposition to violence against Jews, emphasizing that his strictures were exclusively of an economic and cultural nature. While there is plenty of concrete evidence to justify the Cardinal's views, the timing of their public expression was rather unfortunate.

For many Poles, the brutalizing impact of the Depression exposed more acutely than before their deep resentment of manifestations of Jewish polonophobia. For instance, large parts of the Jewish press, together with many Jewish political leaders and

Jewish groups, had adopted a critical stance *vis-à-vis* the Polish state, which often extended to scathing ridicule or denigration of the state and of Poles' cherished beliefs in religion, family and patriotism. The *Bund* and some Zionist groups were especially culpable in this regard. The Jews were perceived to be constantly agitating against things Polish, always demanding more and more while never being grateful for what was done to improve their situation. Nothing, it seemed, was ever enough to satisfy them because most of them were inherently and irrevocably anti-Polish, especially as the *Bund* and the Zionists grew in strength. The Jews appeared to always exaggerate their problems, blaming the Poles, from whom they none the less kept their distance.[34]

Despite the increase in bad feeling between the two communities in the few years before the war, it is noteworthy that Poland did not enact any anti-Semitic legislation, as happened in contemporary Germany, Italy, Romania and Hungary, while in some other countries still, such as France, anti-Semitism was undoubtedly more widespread and organized than in Poland. The perverse view that only the advent of war prevented the enactment of anti-Semitic legislation in Poland[35] comes perilously close to extending to Poles the controversial 'Goldhagan thesis', accordingly to which hatred of Jews was so deeply entrenched among ordinary Germans even before Hitler's advent to power in 1933 that the extermination of the Jews by the Nazi regime during the Second World War was the predictable culmination of this violent, eliminationist type of anti-Semitism in Germany.[36] Although there were a number of notorious episodes in Poland where several Jews were killed, as, for example, in Przytk and Mińsk Mazowiecki in Spring 1936, Polish anti-Semitism was conspicuously devoid of serious violence.[37] Indeed, the most alarming outbreaks of violence invariably resulted from workers' and peasant protests that got out of hand, as in August 1937, during the course of a ten-day strike by the peasantry in southern Poland, when 42 were killed in clashes with police. The Jews, like every other group, enjoyed, in theory, the full protection of the law and constitution, and suffered no more or less than anyone else from their imperfections in practice. At the same time, anti-Semitism *per se* did not become a major political issue before 1939.

The claims of wide-ranging discrimination and persecution of Jews also sit uncomfortably with the fact that in many of the most important spheres of national life, Jews had the opportunity to make an important, if not a pioneering contribution. Among the most significant industrialists were the Jewish families Kronenberg, Natanson, Kon, Poznański, Bloch, Epstein, Rotwand and Wawelberg. Rafael Szereszewski, the financier, was one of the richest men in Poland, and most of the banks and insurance houses were Jewish-owned. The world-famous School of Mathematics at the Jan Kazimierz University in Lwów was staffed mainly by Jews – Hugo Steinhaus, Stanisław Ulam, Stanisław Mazur and Stefan Banach. The leading specialists in law, medicine and economics included Professors Maurycz Allerhand, Rafal Taubenschlag, Leon Berenson, Marceli Handelsman and Ludwik Hirszfeld. Leon Schiller was widely recognized as Poland's best theatre director, while in literature and poetry Julian Tuwim, Antoni Słonimski, Bruno Schulz, Marian Hemar, Józef Wittlin and Bolesław Leśmian were outstanding. In addition to national political figures such as Herman Lieberman, Adolf Gross, Adam Pragier, Feliks Perl and Herman Diamand, and senators Bolesław Motz, Stanisław Posner and Adam Czerniaków, Jews were to be found at the highest-levels of the Army (General Bernard Mond, who was given the honour of organizing the funeral of Marshal Piłsudski), the historical profession (Professor Szymon Askenazy), the Foreign Ministry (Ambassador Jan Ciechanowski) and many other fields: the evidence is copious and incontrovertible. Consequently, it is no exaggeration to affirm that pre-war Poland was home to the largest, most dynamic and most creative Jewish community in Europe, experiencing in a mere twenty years a thoroughgoing process of social and political modernization.[38]

The Polish government's main answer to the perceived 'Jewish Question' was to encourage mass voluntary emigration, partly in association with the Revisionist Zionists of Vladimir Jabotinsky, though it never came up with a proposal that was remotely practicable.[39] Tellingly, when in October 1938 Germany expelled 15,000 Jews who had Polish citizenship, the Polish authorities, unlike the Western democracies, took pity and allowed them to cross the border, where they received assistance despite Poland's many other financial commitments at that time.[40] Nor was Polish public and political opinion as comprehensively hostile to the Jews as has so often been made out. The left wing of the PPS, the outlawed Communist Party of Poland (KPP), the radical wing of the Peasant Party (SL), the Democratic Party (SD), many trade unions, the liberal wing of the *Sanacja*, some Catholic intellectual circles, and the progressive intelligentsia, especially in Warsaw, voiced their disgust of anti-Semitism and their resolve to defend Jewish rights.[41] One of the most dramatic gestures was made by Professor Stanisław Kulczyński when he resigned the Rectorship of the University in Lwów in protest at the introduction of 'ghetto benches' for Jewish students.[42] A petition was signed by 150 prominent academics and intellectuals in protest at anti-Semitic measures in institutions of higher learning. Rudnicki is correct in saying, therefore, that 'a considerable part of Polish society remained immune to the [anti-Semitic] propaganda'.[43]

On the eve of the Second World War anti-Semitism in Poland, and its concomitant, polonophobia, were, on a comparative international scale, and measured against other internal factors in Poland, moderate and limited in scope, as already acknowledged by several historians.[44] And, as Hitler threatened, both phenomena declined in intensity. Anti-Semitic articles in the press appeared far less frequently, as did anti-Semitic sentiment and incidents in the country in general, and Jews contributed handsomely to the National Defence Fund. Of the 150,000 Jews who fought in the Polish Armed Forces against the invading Germans, 32,000 lost their lives.[45] Whatever their differences, and many remained unresolved, most Poles and Jews kept them within a certain perspective. Centuries of living alongside one another had bred an underlying, if rarely revealed, element of mutual respect and comprehension. It is quite unconvincing to claim, therefore, that in September 1939 the Jews of Poland stood on the 'edge of destruction' (Heller) because of Polish anti-Semitism. Rather, their fate resulted from developments during the war, the most deadly of which had nothing whatsoever to do with the character or ethos of the Second Republic or with the Poles themselves as a whole.

NOTES

1. Lucy Dawidowicz, *The War Against the Jews, 1933–45* (Penguin, London, 1975), pp. 472 f.; Ezra Mendelsohn, *Zionism in Poland. The Formative Years, 1915–1926* (Yale University Press, New Haven, Conn., 1981), pp. 1, 2; Pawel Korzec, *Juifs en Pologne. La question juive pendant l'entre-deux-guerres* (Paris, 1980), p. 282; Joshua A. Fishman (ed.), *Studies on Polish Jewry, 1919–1939: The Interplay of Social, Economic and Political Factors in the Struggle of a Minority for its Existence* (Yivo Institute for Jewish Research, New York, 1974), pp. 4–9. For the broader picture, see Martin Gilbert, *The Holocaust: The Jewish Tragedy* (Collins, Glasgow, 1986); Raul Hilberg, *The Destruction of the European Jews* (Holmes & Meier, New York, 1985, 3 vols); and Abraham J. Edelheit and Hershel Edelheit, *History of the Holocaust: A Handbook and Dictionary* (Westview Press, Boulder, Co., 1995).

2. William W. Hagen, 'On the "Final Solution" as a Central European Event: a Comparative Approach to German and Polish Anti-Semitism, 1914–1939', *German History*, 11 (1993), No. 2; Michael Burleigh and Wolfgang Wippermann, *The Racial State: Germany, 1933–1945* (Cambridge University Press, 1991); Philippe Burrin, *Hitler and the Jews. The Genesis of the Holocaust* (Edward Arnold, London, 1994).

3. Celia S. Heller, *On the Edge of Destruction: Jews of Poland Between the Two World Wars* (Columbia University Press, New York, 1977), p. 281.

4. Warsaw's population was 45 per cent Jewish in November 1918, 35 per cent two years later, and 29.1 per cent of 1.29 million in 1939, according to Edward D Wynot, *Warsaw Between the World Wars: Profile of the Capital City in a Developing Land, 1918–1939* (Boulder, Co., 1983), p. 39, and *idem*, 'The Society of Interwar Warsaw', *East European Quarterly*, 7 (1973), No 4, p. 515. See also Ezra Mendelsohn, *The Jews of East Central Europe Between the World Wars* (Indiana University Press, Bloomington, 1983), pp. 23–4; Julian K. Janczak, 'The National Structure of the Population in Łódź in the Years 1820–1939', *Polin*, 6. (1991), pp. 20 ff.; Wiesław Puś, 'The Development of the City of Łódź (1820–1939)', *Polin*, 6 (1991), pp. 3–19.

5. Celia S. Heller, 'Poles of Jewish Background: The Case of Assimilation Without Integration in Interwar Poland', in Fishman, *op. cit.*, pp. 242–76.

6. An interesting and generally even-handed account of how both communities responded to one another in a typical shtetl, Brańsk in Eastern Poland, is Eva Hoffman, *Shtetl: The Life and Death of a Small Town and the World of Polish Jews* (Secker, London, 1997). See also Annamaria Orla-Bukowska, 'Shtetl Communities: Another Image', *Polin*, 8 (1994), pp. 89–113.

7. Ezra Mendelsohn, 'Jewish Politics in Interwar Poland', in Yisrael Gutman, Ezra Mendelsohn, Jehuda Reinharz and Chone Shmeruk (eds), *The Jews of Poland Between Two World Wars* (University Press of New England, Hanover, 1989), pp. 9–19; Gershon C. Bacon, 'Agudat Israel in Interwar Poland', *ibid.*, pp. 20–35.

8. Magdalena M. Opalski and Israel Bartal, *Poles and Jews: A Failed Brotherhood* (University Press of New England, Hanover, 1993).

9. Władysław T. Bartoszewski, 'Poles and Jews as the "Other"', *Polin*, 4 (1989), pp. 6–17.

10. Peter D. Stachura, 'National Identity and the Ethnic Minorities in Early Interwar Poland', in Peter D. Stachura (ed.), *Poland Between the Wars, 1918–1939* (Macmillan, London, 1998).

11. Mark Levene, *War, Jews and the New Europe: The Diplomacy of Lucien Wolf, 1914–1919* (Oxford University Press, 1992), and *idem*, 'Britain, a British Jew, and Jewish Relations with the New Poland: The Making of the Polish Minorities Treaty of 1919', *Polin*, 8 (1994), pp. 14–41; Eugene C. Black, 'Lucien Wolf and Making of Poland: Paris, 1919', *Polin*, 2 (1987), pp. 5–36; Andrzej Kapiszewski (ed.), *Hugh Gibson and a Controversy over Polish–Jewish Relations after World War I: A Documentary History* (Jagiellonian University Press, Kraków, 1991). Gibson was the first American minister to be appointed (April 1919) to independent Poland.

12. W. F. Reddaway, *Marshal Piłsudski* (Routledge, London, 1939), p. 140. Details of the war in Norman Davies, *White Eagle, Red Star: The Polish-Soviet War, 1919–20* (Macdonald, London, 1972), and Adam Zamoyski, *The Battle for the Marchlands* (Columbia University Press, New York, 1981).

13. Jędrzej Giertych, *In Defence of My Country* (privately published, London, 1980), p. 279.

14. Peter D. Stachura, 'The Battle of Warsaw, August 1920, and the Development of the Second Polish Republic', in Stachura (ed.), *Poland Between the Wars*, *op. cit.*

15. Pawel Korzec, 'Das Abkommen zwischen der Regierung Grabski und der jüdischen Parlaments-Vertretung', *Jahrbücher für Geschichte Osteuropas*, 20 (1972), No. 3, pp. 331–66.

16. Mendelsohn, *Zionism in Poland*, pp. 130 ff., 213 ff., 300 ff.

17. Frank Golczewski, 'The Problem of Sunday Rest in Interwar Poland', in Gutman *et al.* (eds), *The Jews of Poland*, pp. 158–72.

18. Joseph Marcus, *Social and Political History of the Jews in Poland, 1919–1939* (Mouton, New York, 1983), pp. 41, 66, 190.

19. Jacek M. Majchrowski, 'Some Observations on the Situation of the Jewish Minority in Poland during the Years 1918–1939', *Polin*, 3 (1988), pp. 307–8.

20. Wacław Jędrzejewicz, *Piłsudski: A Life for Poland* (Hippocrene Books, New York, 1982), p. 248; Harry M. Rabinowicz, *The Legacy of Polish Jewry: A History of Polish Jews in the Inter-war Years, 1919–1939* (Thomas Voseloff, New York, 1965), p. 56; Bela Vago

and George L. Mosse (eds), *Jews and Non-Jews in Eastern Europe, 1918–1945* (Transaction Books, New Jersey, 1974), pp. 211–12.

21. Andrzej Chojnowski, 'The Jewish Question in the Work of the *Instytut Badań Spraw Narodowościowych* in Warsaw', *Polin*, 4 (1989), pp. 159–68.

22. Edward D. Wynot, 'Polish–Jewish Relations, 1918–1939: An Overview', in Dennis J. Dunn (ed.), *Religion and Nationalism in Eastern Europe and the Soviet Union* (Lynne Rienner Publishers, Boulder, Co., 1987), pp. 25 ff.

23. Zbigniew Landau and Jerzy Tomaszewski, *The Polish Economy in the Twentieth Century* (Routledge, London, 1985), pp. 90–109; Jack J. Taylor, *The Economic Development of Poland, 1919–1950* (Cornell University Press, Ithaca, 1952), pp. 139–53.

24. Benefit covered enterprises employing at least five persons, whereas most unemployed Jews had been either self-employed or attached to a very small workshop.

25. The taxation system was heavily weighted towards the towns, where an overwhelming majority of Jews lived. They paid up to 40 per cent of national taxes, despite constituting only about 10 per cent of the population. See Simon Segal, *The New Poland and the Jews* (Lee Furman, New York, 1938), p. 141.

26. Zosa Szajkowski, 'Western Jewish Aid and Intervention for Polish Jewry, 1919–1939', in Fishman (ed.), *Studies on Polish Jewry*, pp. 150–241.

27. Raphael Mahler, 'Jews in Public Service and the Liberal Professions in Poland, 1918–1939', *Jewish Social Studies*, 6 (1944), No. 4, pp. 294–308, 318 ff.

28. Marcus, *Social and Political History*, pp. 247, 254 ff.

29. Edward D. Wynot, *Polish Politics in Transition: The Camp of National Unity and the Struggle for Power, 1935–1939* (University of Georgia Press, Athens, Georgia, 1974), *passim*; Adam Bromke, *The Meaning and Uses of Polish History* (Columbia University Press, New York, 1987), *passim*.

30. Emanuel Melzer, 'Antisemitism in the Last Years of the Second Polish Republic', in Gutman *et al.* (eds), *The Jews of Poland*, p. 134; Karol Grünberg, 'The Atrocities Against the Jews in the Third Reich as seen by the National-Democratic Press (1933–39)', *Polin*, 5 (1990), pp. 103–13; Anna Landau-Czajka, 'The Ubiquitous Enemy: The Jew in the Political Thought of Radical Right-Wing Nationalists in Poland, 1926–39', *Polin*, 4 (1989), pp. 169–203; Szymon Rudnicki, *Obóz Narodowo Radykalny. Geneza i Działalność* (Czytelnik, Warsaw, 1985); Jacek M. Majchrowski, *Silni, zwarci, gotowi. Myśl polityczna Obozu Zjednoczenia Narodowego* (Warsaw, 1985).

31. Szymon Rudnicki, 'Ritual Slaughter as a Political Issue', *Polin*, 7 (1992), pp. 147–60.

32. Szymon Rudnicki, 'From "Numerus Clausus" to "Numerus Nullus"', *Polin*, 2 (1987), pp. 246–68.

33. R. Modras, *The Catholic Church and Antisemitism: Poland, 1933–1939* (Harwood Academic, New York, 1994); Franciszek Adamski, 'The Jewish Question in Polish Religious Periodicals in the Second Republic: The Case of the Przegląd katolicki', *Polin*, 8 (1994), pp. 129–45; Edward D. Wynot, 'The Catholic Church and the Polish State, 1935–1939', *Journal of Church and State*, 15 (1973), pp. 223–40.

34. Ezra Mendelsohn, 'Interwar Poland: good for the Jews or bad for the Jews?', in Chimen Abramsky, Maciej Jachimczyk and Antony Polonsky (eds), *The Jews in Poland* (Basil Blackwell, Oxford, 1986), pp. 130–46.

35. Rafael F. Scharf, 'In Anger and In Sorrow: Towards a Polish–Jewish Dialogue', *Polin*, 1 (1986), p. 272.

36. David Goldhagen, *Hitler's Willing Executioners: Ordinary Germans and the Holocaust* (London, 1996).

37. Adam Penkalla, 'The "Przytk Incidents" of 9 March 1936 from Archival Documents', *Polin*, 5 (1990), pp. 327–59; Richard M. Watt, *Bitter Glory: Poland and Its Fate, 1918 to 1939* (Simon & Schuster, New York, 1979), p. 364.

38. Mendelsohn, 'Interwar Poland: good for the Jews or bad for the Jews?', p. 139; Norman Davies, *God's Playground: A History of Poland, Volume II: 1795 to the Present* (Clarendon Press, Oxford, 1981), p. 407.

39. Full coverage in Lawrence Weinbaum, *A Marriage of Convenience: The New Zionist Organization and the Polish Government, 1936–1939* (Columbia University Press, New York, 1993); Howard Rosenblum, 'Promoting an International Conference to Solve the Jewish Problem: the New Zionist Organization's Alliance with Poland, 1938–1939', *The Slavonic and East European Review*, 69 (1991), No. 3, pp. 478–501; Jerzy Tomaszewski, 'Vladimir Jabotinsky's Talks with Representatives of the Polish Government', *Polin*, 3 (1988), pp. 276–93. The Polish government secretly helped an indeterminate number of Jews to reach Palestine through Romania, in defiance of British controls.

40. Marcus, *Social and Political History*, p. 380; Karol Jonca, 'The Expulsion of Polish Jews from the Third Reich in 1938', *Polin*, 8 (1994), pp. 255–81; Hardi Swarsensky, 'Transport nach Polen (1938)', *Bulletin des Leo Baeck Instituts*, 81 (1988), No. 1, pp. 27–30.

41. Jerzy Holzer, 'Relations between Polish and Jewish left-wing groups in interwar Poland', in Abramsky *et al.* (eds), *Jews in Poland*, pp. 140–46; *idem*, 'Polish Political Parties and Antisemitism', *Polin*, 8 (1994), pp. 194–205; Aharon Weiss, 'The Activities of the Democratic Societies and Democratic Party in Defending Jewish Rights in Poland on the Eve of Hitler's Invasion', *Polin*, 7 (1992), pp. 260–67; Władysław Bartoszewski, 'Some Thoughts on Polish–Jewish Relations', *Polin*, 1 (1986), p. 279; Barbara Wachowska, 'Łódź Remained Red: Elections to the City Council of 27 September 1936', *Polin*, 9 (1996) pp. 83–106.

42. His letter of resignation of 11 January 1938 is reproduced in English in Manfred Kridl, Józef Wittlin and Władysław Malinowski, *The Democratic Heritage of Poland* (Allen & Unwin, London, 1944), pp. 173–4.
43. Rudnicki, 'Ritual Slaughter', p. 147.
44. Władysław Bartoszewski, 'Polish–Jewish Relations in Occupied Poland, 1939–1945', in Abramsky *et al.* (eds) *Jews in Poland*, p. 148; Davies, *God's Playground*, II, pp. 260 ff., 408 f.; Mendelsohn, in Abramsky *et al.* (eds), pp. 138–9.
45. Rabinowicz, *Legacy of Polish Jewry*, p. 168.

4 Władysław Sikorski: Soldier, Politician and Statesman, 1881–1943

With little more than fifty years since the death of General Władysław Sikorski in an air crash off Gibraltar on 4 July 1943, it is perhaps appropriate to reflect on the historical role of one of the most controversial Polish leaders of modern times. Like other prominent Poles who combined a political and military career, such as Marshal Józef Piłsudski, Sikorski has attracted as many critics as admirers, and the passage of half a century has scarcely diminished the intensity of debate about him both in Poland and in the Polish diaspora. His performance as leader of the so-called Polish Government-in-Exile from 1939 until 1943 in particular has been the subject of sharp exchanges. But while it is not surprising that this final, crucial period of his career should have received so much attention, it should not be overlooked that even before the tragic outcome of the September Campaign of 1939 resulted in his premiership Sikorski had already emerged as a well-known and substantial public figure during the period of the Second Polish Republic. Stepping into the limelight of Polish and international politics in 1939 represented for him, albeit in circumstances he could hardly have anticipated or desired, the realization of a long-standing ambition to lead his country once again, as he had done briefly in the early 1920s.

Born on 20 May 1881 in the small Galician town of Tuszów Narodowy, where his father was a schoolmaster, Sikorski completed his secondary schooling in Rzeszów and went on to take a degree in civil engineering at Lwów Technical University in 1908. In addition, in these early years he developed political and military attitudes which laid the foundations of his subsequent career. His concern to help promote the cause of Polish independence from the three partitioning powers, Tsarist Russia, Germany and Austria-Hungary, led him into active membership of several nationalist and paramilitary organizations prior to the outbreak of the First World War, including the Union of Polish Youth (Zet), the Union for Active Struggle (ZWC) and the Riflemen's Association (PFS). From 1911 he joined with Piłsudski, Marian Kukiel, Kazimierz Sosnkowski and others in planning for an armed uprising in the event of a wider European war, with the aim of establishing an independent Polish national state. By that time Sikorski's political outlook had shifted from a flirtation with the ultra-nationalist National Democratic movement to a more positive identification with liberalism.[1] In November 1910 he was a co-founder in Lwów of the Polish Progressive Party (*Polskie Stronnictwo Postępowe*).[2] His appointment two years later as head of the military department of the Commission of Confederated Independence Parties in Galicia was further evidence of his determination to pursue both political and military activities. Sikorski's endorsement of the 'trialist concept', that the Polish question should be resolved within a Habsburg framework, was the genesis of his later estrangement from Piłsudski who, self-consciously carrying on the Romantic-insurrectionist tradition of 1830 and 1863, considered it imperative for Polish military strength to play the key part in the creation of a new Polish state.[3] Sikorski made an important contribution to the setting up in August 1914 of the Supreme National Committee (NKN), a coordinating body representing all the Polish political parties in Galicia which claimed to be the nucleus of a future Polish national government. As chief of its military department from 1914 to 1916, he was regarded along with Stanisław Kot as constituting the organization's more pronouncedly democratic element.[4] The NKN espoused the trialist concept, which remained Sikorski's preferred solution to the national issue until the last year of the war. In the meantime, he helped form the Polish Legions and went on to hold a number of senior command posts in them.[5] His relations with Piłsudski, commander of the Legions' First Brigade, began to deteriorate from 1915–16, not only over the nature of the struggle for independence, but also over the future of the NKN and the Legions.[6]

The dispute was effectively settled by the course of the war in 1917–18, particularly as the implications of the Bolshevik

Revolution in Russia and the conclusion of the Treaty of Brest-Litovsk in March 1918 began to exert a significant influence on developments. Russia withdrew from the conflict, while other political and territorial provisions of the treaty that were disadvantageous to the Polish cause put an abrupt end to the trialist notion. Sikorski resigned from the Austro-Hungarian army in protest at the treaty, was interned in Hungary, court-martialled and then released in the chaos which accompanied the collapse of the Habsburg Empire in autumn 1918. Emerging from the war a battle-hardened soldier and a somewhat chastened but wiser politician, Colonel Sikorski was exactly the type of personality whose talents the Polish Republic needed to engage if its newly won independence was not to be the ephemeral phenomenon many Western observers were predicting.

Sikorski, an intelligent, able and energetic personality, was eager for professional and social advancement. He possessed many of the qualities which characterized the Polish Army officer of the inter-war era, including toughness, bravery and integrity. A staunch patriot who constantly emphasized his Catholic and anti-Communist views, Sikorski was already noted in 1918 for his prodigious vanity, which led him to affect gentry descent and to see himself as a man of destiny. Although his private life as husband (he married Helena Zubczewska in 1909) and father of a daughter, Zofia, was happy, his reserved and somewhat aloof demeanour meant that he did not easily make friends. Personal relationships were based invariably on mutual respect rather than genuine warmth. In later life, his haughtiness too often gave way to arrogance, and his increasingly autocratic manner provoked resentment among colleagues.

In the period 1918–21, Poland had to endure a desperate fight for survival against overwhelming odds. Confronted by an economy devastated by war, rebellious ethnic minorities and the most rudimentary administrative, judicial, financial and political structures, the country had few friends and a multitude of enemies. Its existence could not have been more precarious in November 1918, especially as its frontiers had still to be definitively drawn and recognized. The Treaty of Versailles had indeed demarcated most of Poland's western border, but in the East the situation had been left open, thus creating an immediate source of conflict with the Ukrainians, Lithuanians and Russians.[7] Through a series of wars the Poles did finally assert the territorial integrity of their state, thanks principally to the endeavours of the army, among whose leaders was Sikorski.

As Chief of Staff in Galicia, Sikorski played a notable role in the successful campaign to secure Eastern Galicia against the Ukrainian nationalist forces in 1918–19, but his finest hour came in the Polish–Soviet War of 1919–20. Promoted Major-General in April 1920, his inspired leadership of the Fifth Army in the Battle of Warsaw in August that year was an indispensable factor in the Polish victory. Although most of the credit for this 'Miracle on the Vistula' has to be accorded to Marshal Piłsudski, Sikorski's skilful improvizations during the Polish counter-offensive that brought victory were of fundamental importance. A few weeks later, he took command of the Third Army and destroyed the '*Konarmiya*', the much-feared Russian cavalry army, at the Battle of Komarów, near Zamość.[8] For these triumphs, which preserved Poland as an independent state within the international order laid down by the Treaty of Versailles, and which also prevented the incursion of revolutionary Soviet Bolshevism into the heart of Europe, Sikorski's military reputation was second only to that of Piłsudski. He had demonstrated in unequivocal fashion that he was an outstanding military strategist and frontline commander.[9] At the age of 39, Sikorski was rightly celebrated as a national hero. But rather than being the crowning point of a career, his achievements were merely the overture to a high-profile progression to the status of an archetypal political general. As for other officers of the day, the broader context was provided by the exalted status the Polish Army enjoyed in society for its victories in 1918–21, particularly for its defeat of the Soviet Bolsheviks. The Polish Republic itself gained immeasurably in self-confidence, and began to tackle its many problems with renewed vigour.[10]

Appointed Chief of the General Staff of the Polish Armed Forces with the rank of Lieutenant-General in April 1921, Sikorski was required to show a deep understanding of military needs as well as a sensitivity to the political implications of the Army's role in peacetime. Past differences with the Head of State and

Supreme Army Commander, Piłsudski, were set aside as both men strove to work together in the national interest. Sikorski's organizational abilities and talent for judicious delegation of work to subordinates made for a successful tenure of office, which was cut short only by a major political crisis towards the end of 1922.

The system of parliamentary democracy in Poland, of which Sikorski was a supporter, though he stressed the need for a strong executive that could overcome party obstructionism, never attained stability.[11] The greed and inexperience of politicians on all sides bred corruption, while many political parties acted selfishly and irresponsibly. Petty sectional interests were too frequently pursued to the neglect of the national interest. Against this inauspicious background, the first presidential election in the Republic brought political passions to a head in December 1922, when Gabriel Narutowicz was elected, thanks in part to the votes cast for him by the National Minorities' Bloc led by the Zionist, Yitshak Gruenbaum. The nationalist Right denigrated Narutowicz as a 'Jewish president'. The campaign of vilification against him reached a climax on 16 December when he was assassinated in Warsaw by an ultra-nationalist. The shock and revulsion occasioned by this episode brought Poland to the verge of civil war. Apart from domestic dangers, Poland's enemies, and above all Germany and Soviet Russia, were always likely to try to take advantage of such a crisis. Firm government capable of adopting measures to calm the situation was urgently demanded.

General Sikorski, who was not affiliated to any political party at this time and could therefore be relied upon to act impartially, was called in to head a non-Party cabinet as Prime Minister. He also assumed the office of Minister of the Interior. For the second time within only a few years, he found himself performing the role of national saviour, and as before he successfully executed his responsibilities. Calling for national unity and vigilance on the borders,[12] he quickly re-established law and order and reduced the political temperature to manageable proportions. Sikorski then revealed a constructive approach in several other important spheres. Preparatory work on the building of the new Baltic port of Gdynia was accelerated,[13] and consultations with experts regarding necessary financial reform were initiated at his instigation.

In due course Gdynia developed as one of the outstanding achievements of the inter-war Polish economy, and a later Prime Minister, Władysław Grabski, was able to introduce a new currency, the *zloty*, and set up the Bank of Poland.[14] Finally, in March 1923, Sikorski was greatly encouraged when the Conference of Ambassadors decided to recognize Poland's frontiers with Lithuania and the Soviet Union that had been drawn by the Treaty of Riga at the conclusion of the Polish–Soviet War two years previously. A delighted Prime Minister was able to inform parliament (*Sejm*) on 16 March that 'Polish Wilno, twice wrenched from the barbarians by the efforts of our soldiers, belongs forever to the Motherland, and ancient Polish Lwów, together with Little Eastern Poland, will share the fate and glory of the Polish nation for all time'.[15]

Although Prime Minister for only a brief period, from 16 December 1922 to 26 May 1923, Sikorski used the experience to fine-tune his political philosophy. Having incurred the lasting enmity of the National Democrats for proposing a tax on higher incomes,[16] he became contemptuous of that party's vociferous chauvinism and anti-Semitism. For those outside the nationalist camp, however, Sikorski's essentially moderate views were still regarded with suspicion. Thus the Jewish lobby was alienated when he recalled the pro-Soviet attitude of a not inconsiderable number of Polish Jews in the war of 1919–20 as evidence of their basic disloyalty towards the Polish state, and exacerbated the situation by affirming that Poland's future had to be decided by the Catholic majority.[17] His relations with the Jewish community were further damaged when, in 1923, he ordered the expulsion from Poland of some 12,000 Jews who had fled the Russian civil war.[18] He considered them illegal immigrants and reminded his critics that Poland had already since 1918 granted citizenship to over 600,000 Jewish refugees from Russia. In view of the unsettled social and economic situation in Poland at that time, he reasoned that another large influx simply could not be absorbed. None the less, the Zionists and their allies denounced his government as anti-Semitic.[19]

Sikorski's premiership was undoubtedly crucial to the early development of independent Poland. Many other crises lay ahead, but he had shown that these could be efficaciously dealt with on the basis of an iron will and ambition to succeed. On a more personal level, the experience of high office, besides sharpening his political outlook, bolstered his belief that he was a natural leader of the nation. It is noteworthy that in December 1922 Piłsudski remarked on Sikorski's 'great ambition' while praising his ability, and recommended him for higher posts of command. In autumn 1923, Sikorski was appointed Inspector General of the Infantry.[20]

The relationship between Piłsudski and Sikorski had never been warm, despite their close collaboration before the First World War and during its early stages. Piłsudski had his own small and exclusive circle of advisers, and Sikorski preferred to keep very much to himself. Over time, their political views diverged on a number of important issues, while the factionalism of the officer corps in the Polish Army, which was particularly apparent before the May Coup in 1926, drove both men further apart. Sikorski's secret group, 'Honour and Fatherland' (*Honor i Ojczyzna*), was one such faction that existed, allegedly on Masonic lines, in the Army from 1921 to 1925.[21] But in the early 1920s there was still a good deal of mutual respect and admiration, and they could work together. Piłsudski might also have been impressed by Sikorski's formation in 1925 of a Frontier Defence Corps in response to the menace of Bolshevik terrorist bands in the East,[22] had it not been for the bitter dispute that arose over the matter of the accountability of the highest army authorities.

As Minister of War in Władysław Grabski's cabinet (February 1924–November 1925), Sikorski proposed, with cabinet approval and in the form of a draft bill to parliament on 14 March 1924, that a Council for the Defence of the State be set up in wartime under civilian political control. Piłsudski, for whom the Army was a sacred institution, victorious in battle and the ultimate guarantor of Poland's independence and integrity, rejected any attempt that would render it susceptible to political interference and intrigue. He rounded on Sikorski in scathing terms, insisting on the complete autonomy of the Army Command.[23] Sikorski protested that he was upholding the rights of the parliamentary state in a vital area of national interest, and offered a compromise.

This was also flatly rejected because it retained the principle of ultimate political control by the Minister of War and parliament. The issue rumbled on without resolution during Sikorski's term of office. His proposal was subsequently withdrawn by his successor as Minister of War, General Lucjan Żeligowski, on 4 May 1926.[24] The relationship between Piłsudski and Sikorski was finally and irrevocably broken, however, and the two erstwhile colleagues became bitter enemies. Consequently, the Marshal's *coup d'état* in May 1926 not only settled this particular bone of contention on his terms, it also marked the effective end of Sikorski's military and political career in the Second Republic.

Sikorski had not retained his post in the new cabinet led by Count Aleksander Skrzyński that came into office at the end of 1925. Instead, he had been appointed commander of the Lwów Military District. In that capacity, he adopted a broadly neutral stance during the May coup, helping neither Piłsudski nor the government.[25] It is possible that he was calculating that those confused days might somehow turn to his advantage.[26] What really mattered was that, as a result of the coup's success, Sikorski was a marked man. As a matter of political expediency, Piłsudski could not afford to dismiss him immediately, but he took steps to have Sikorski watched at his post in Lwów until the appropriate moment for decisive action arrived. That came with the government party's (BBWR – Nonparty Bloc for Cooperation with the Government) relative success at the national elections in March 1928, when it won over 25 per cent of the vote against 8.6 per cent for the Right, 10 per cent for the Centre and 26 per cent for the Left.[27]

Piłsudski could now afford to dispense with Sikorski's services, thus exacting revenge for the army command issue and at the same time ridding himself of his only potential rival in terms of authority and popular prestige.[28] Sikorski was removed from his post a few days later, but was retained on the reserve list, where he languished throughout the remainder of the Republic's lifetime. Sikorski and the *Sanacja*, the name meaning literally 'moral cleansing' which was commonly used to describe the post-1926 Piłsudski regime, were totally incompatible. A leading military historian has interpreted Piłsudski's decision as 'a tacit recognition of the fact that there was no suitable appointment in the armed forces for a former prime minister' who needed, in any case, like other officers, 'a long sabbatical'.[29] Nevertheless, it is regrettable that a soldier of Sikorski's stature should have been denied the opportunity for the next eleven years of serving his country in an increasingly tense international atmosphere. The episode bears rather sad testimony to the self-destructive internecine feuding among Poland's élite at that time.

In what amounted to semi-retirement from March 1928, Sikorski pursued his interest in military-strategic affairs and defined more precisely his political stance. Spending much of the period from 1928 to 1932 abroad, mostly in France and Switzerland, he made use of his contacts in the upper echelons of the French Army to keep abreast of the latest developments in military theory. The eventual result was a major publication in 1934, which was subsequently translated into French and English.[30] In this study, which put him in the front rank of contemporary military theorists, Sikorski painted an uncannily accurate picture of the nature of future warfare, which would involve mobile operations by substantial armoured and mechanized armies, backed up by air power. Within the scenario of mechanized warfare he emphasized the vital contribution to be made by the high-speed tank, which would spearhead bold and rapid manoeuvres. The importance of strategic surprise and flexibility was also held to be crucial. Sikorski considered the Polish Army obsolete, but his views found little resonance in the military establishment.[31]

It was perhaps inevitable that Sikorski's political outlook from 1928 to 1939 should have been influenced to some extent by personal rancour at his treatment by Piłsudski. In addition, however, he developed a principled opposition to the increasingly authoritarian and anti-democratic nature of the Marshal's regime.[32] National security and foreign affairs were his specialist areas of interest. An unabashed francophile, he was convinced of the virtues of the Franco-Polish alliance despite certain manifestations of growing French indifference, and vigorously opposed Foreign Minister Józef Beck's preference for playing down the French connection in favour of promoting a better understanding with Germany.[33] Sikorski predictably denounced the Polish–German

Non-Aggression Pact of January 1934 as inimical to the national interest.

He further clashed with the government over its unyielding anti-Sovietism, which reflected, of course, Piłsudski's long-standing attitude. Although anti-Communist and a victorious general against the Soviets, Sikorski had developed the conviction from the early 1920s that for her own security Poland ought to seek some form of *rapprochement* with the USSR. This view, which recognized Germany as Poland's inveterate adversary and the Soviet Union as a potential tactical ally, formed an integral element of his thinking on foreign policy to the end of his career.[34] There is no suggestion of his being a 'Red General', for the understanding that he envisaged before 1939 was to be strictly limited and did not involve any acceptance of Communism or Soviet influence in Polish domestic affairs. Rather, the relationship was to be based on their mutual need to oppose German aggression and ambition. From 1933 he consistently spoke out in favour of an alliance with the USSR.

In domestic politics, Sikorski's belief in 'organized democracy' was bound to accentuate his opposition to the *Sanacja*, though he refused to be aligned too closely with a specific ideological posture or political party.[35] Accusations of opportunism by his critics were accordingly plentiful. He regarded himself increasingly as the quintessential non-party patriot with an important mission to safeguard the national interest, as he defined it. With Piłsudski thinking along similar lines, there was clearly no room for both of them on the same stage at the same time. Sikorski was genuinely appalled by what he understood to be the sheer incompetence and corruption of the government during the early 1930s. But he still tried on several occasions to establish a dialogue with some of its leaders, including Walery Sławek, leader of the BBWR, with a view to being reinstated in an official position.[36] These advances came to nothing. They indicate, however, a willingness on Sikorski's part to compromise with a regime which he professed to despise. Possibly he felt that he could improve or help reform it in ways which would have made it more efficient and acceptable. In any case, his attitude in the early 1930s suggests a sense of frustration and impotence at his continued exclusion from the corridors of power. It was only when his efforts at reconciliation had been totally rebuffed that Sikorski moved into more outspokenly public opposition.

Following his return from abroad to Poland in 1932, Sikorski gradually set about making contact with various well-known political figures who, like him, had fallen out of favour with the government. Ignacy Paderewski, the world-famous pianist and former Prime Minister (1919), the Silesian hero, Wojciech Korfanty, the leading Peasant Party personality, Wincenty Witos, and General Józef Haller were among those with whom he associated on the moderate Right and Centre of the political spectrum. They were united in wanting a restoration of parliamentary democracy in Poland and a reaffirmation of a pro-French orientation in foreign policy. Sikorski's efforts to provide organizational coherence to these views, however, met with clear failure.

A campaign in support of Paderewski's candidacy for the Presidency in 1933 proved abortive, while the clandestine Union for the Rebirth of the Republic (ZORz), whose aim was to topple the regime, suffered the same fate.[37] Sikorski did not have an organized, popular base of support, and no amount of political intrigue could compensate for that. At the same time there was no-one in Poland in the early 1930s who could hope successfully to challenge even an ailing Piłsudski, whose charismatic presence obscured the deficiencies of his government. More importantly, Poland had come a long way from the problems that had prompted the coup of 1926. Although the impact of the Depression was severe, with rapidly rising unemployment, falling living standards and renewed ethnic tensions, especially with the Jews, under Piłsudski's overlordship the country had developed a remarkable resilience and vitality at home and a considerable status in the international arena. Consequently, domestic opponents such as Sikorski were bound to flounder sooner rather than later. It was only after Piłsudski's death in May 1935 and the subsequent failure of the regime to fill the political lacuna that Polish politics offered some scope for dissenting voices to be heard by a potentially wider audience. Even so, Sikorski soon discovered the limitations of what could be achieved.

When a final effort to reach an understanding with the moderate circles of the post-Piłsudski regime failed, Sikorski made a concerted attempt to organize an opposition movement on the basis of his ties with the moderate Right and Centre. The resultant 'Front Morges' in February 1936, named after Paderewski's Swiss villa where it was formed, was largely influenced by Sikorski's political and ideological outlook.[38] A western-style parliamentary democracy and a pro-French foreign policy linked to limited cooperation with the Soviet Union was to be underpinned by a variety of important domestic reforms, including a modernization of the army. A capitalist economic system was endorsed, in which private property was protected and state interventionism reduced to a minimum, while the resurgent 'Jewish question' was to be tackled through a voluntary programme of mass emigration of Jews. How this programme was to be implemented in practice was not specified, intimating perhaps that its inclusion in the Front's manifesto was in hasty response to the contemporary debate in Polish society about the position of the Jews. Finally, the Front promised a combative stance towards Communism and the sustenance of Christian values.

The Polish public did not take the Front seriously. There were presentational difficulties, but, more tellingly, it was composed of too many disparate elements to be a credible alternative. For example, how realistic was it to expect politicians ranging from the socialist Herman Lieberman to the conservative Peasant Party stalwart Stanisław Mikołajczyk to work together? Their strongest, perhaps only, point of unity was a basic desire to bring down the government at the earliest opportunity. Otherwise, no-one could be certain that the Front would not rapidly disintegrate into its constituent parts. The Front's appeal to the public also failed because it was widely perceived as little more than a vehicle for Sikorski's vaunting ambition, and it attracted only a handful of weak and rather half-hearted political allies, including the Christian Democratic Party and the National Workers' Party. No real improvement to its position occurred when it coalesced with these parties in October 1937 to form the Party of Labour (*Stronnictwo Pracy*) under the leadership of Korfanty, Karol Popiel and General Haller. The party's nationalist, Catholic, democratic and socially conservative programme was virtually identical to that of the Front. Sikorski, however, had become disillusioned with the Front's demise as an independent political initiative, and did not lend the new party much support.[39]

During the last few years before the Second World War, Sikorski withdrew from active politics, partly in disappointment, and partly also in deference to the growing need for national unity in the face of the threatening international situation and the radicalization of Polish society. He probably saw some sense in the broad appeal of the government-sponsored Camp of National Unity (OZON), which was set up as the BBWR's successor in 1937, though he rejected its quasi-fascist and sinister anti-Semitic overtones.[40] On the other hand, he respected the importance of the Army as a symbol of patriotic loyalty. Sikorski had as early as the mid-1930s become convinced that a new European war was only a matter of time, in which Poland's independence would be seriously challenged.[41] These considerations encouraged him to think of himself once again as a soldier rather than a politician. Unfortunately, he had to suffer a final humiliation from an unforgiving regime: a few days before the German invasion on 1 September 1939, Sikorski's offer to serve his country in a military command post was ignored by the Commander-in-Chief of the Polish Armed Forces, Marshal Edward Śmigły-Rydz.

The collapse of the Second Republic in September 1939 ended an unsatisfying phase of Sikorski's career. At the same time, possibilities were created for him to take a new direction, in which the role of soldier and politician was replaced by that of national leader and international statesman. With the pre-war regime discredited by Poland's defeat and its leading officials interned in Romania, the political vacuum could only be filled by someone of Sikorski's calibre. He had reached France in mid-September, but he was not the first choice of Władysław Raczkiewicz, the new President of the Polish Republic that had now transferred its seat to Paris, to lead the Government-in-Exile. However, Stanisław Stroński, a former Nationalist politician who had been associated with Sikorski in the Front Morges, lacked sufficient support to form a cabinet.[42] Somewhat reluctantly, Raczkiewicz, a former high-ranking *Sanacja* official, turned to Sikorski, who accepted the posts of Prime Minister and Minister of Defence on 30 September out of a sense of patriotic duty and belief in his ability to provide good leadership in this profound crisis for Poland. On 7 November he was also appointed Commander-in-Chief of the Polish Armed Forces, thus confirming his status as the most powerful figure in the government. His task was made more daunting still by the unexpected fall of France in June 1940 and the necessary removal of his cabinet to London.[43]

From the outset, Sikorski's government in London was obliged to operate under a number of constraints which boded ill for the Polish cause. In the first instance, his cabinet, which included representatives from the four main pre-war political traditions – socialist, nationalist, populist and labour, as well as *Sanacja* moderates – was bedevilled by bitter squabbling and rivalry. Sikorski repeatedly presented his government as a decisive break from the pre-war regime by stressing its commitment in a restored independent Polish state to parliamentary democracy, social justice and equal rights for minorities,[44] and sought to reassure specifically the Jewish community that it also had a future in that context. To demonstrate his good faith, he encouraged a number of Jews, such as Herman Lieberman and the Zionist leader Ignacy Schwarcbart, to serve on the advisory Polish National Council.[45] In reality, however, political loyalties and attitudes rooted in the pre-war era could not be brushed aside so easily, and members of his government expressed different views on a host of major social, economic and political matters. Considerable tension existed also between his government and the officer corps of the Army, which was largely Piłsudskiite in sentiment. As a major opponent of the revered Marshal before the war, Sikorski was disliked and distrusted by many officers, who also did not take kindly, in the tradition of their hero, to civilian political control. Where unity did exist, however, was on the basic objective of re-establishing an independent Polish state.

Secondly, despite all the external trappings of power, Sikorski's personal position was not entirely secure. President Raczkiewicz and the one-time *Sanacja* Foreign Minister, August Zalewski, moved within a short time from an initially reserved stance to one of outright opposition to some of his policies, especially those concerning the Soviet Union. It also did not help that his choice of advisers was at times unwise, though a number of his appointments in the Army were fully vindicated in due course. Moreover, had Sikorski been a less withdrawn, more approachable personality, he might have been able to better reconcile the divisions in the exiled government and the Polish community in Britain, and thus secure for himself a sounder platform from which to conduct international affairs.

The early precariousness of Sikorski's position was underlined just after his arrival in London in mid-summer 1940, when he was sharply condemned by many of his compatriots for failing to evacuate to safety the bulk of the 80,000 Polish troops which he had commanded in France. When it then became known that he had made friendly overtures to the Russians without proper consultation with his cabinet, an unsuccessful attempt was made, particularly by former adherents of the pre-war regime, to sack him.[46]

The Poles were very much the subordinate partner in the Western alliance. Churchill, who had considerable respect and admiration for Sikorski while finding most of his colleagues tiresome, was not willing to allow Polish interests to impede either those of Britain or of the broader anti-German coalition, especially following the Soviet Union's accession to it in July 1941.[47] It is undeniable that Britain and Poland were unnatural allies; even before 1939 there had been little sympathy and understanding between them. The Poles could recall that for most of the First World War Britain had strongly rejected the idea of an independent Polish state, and that when this attitude changed as a result of the Bolshevik Revolution and American pressure, David Lloyd George made no secret of his anti-Polish bias over the problems of the eastern border, Upper Silesia, East Prussia and Danzig.[48] Together with Lord Halifax, the Foreign Secretary, Lloyd George (now in retirement) had welcomed the Soviet invasion and occupation of Eastern Poland in September 1939. The British socialist and labour movement had adopted a strongly pro-Soviet stance in the Polish–Bolshevik War in 1919–20, and along with Marxist intellectuals and some Jewish spokesmen had continued to evince anti-Polish sentiments throughout the interwar period. Moreover, in October 1938 the British government had condemned Poland's recovery of the predominantly Polish district of Cieszyn from Czechoslovakia, which had abandoned diplomatic negotiation to seize the area at a time of Polish vulnerability in 1919–20.

As a consequence of this sad legacy, Poles can have been under no illusions that the British Guarantee to Poland in March 1939[49] and the Anglo–Polish Pact of Mutual Assistance in August were formulated by Britain in response to the German threat to the European balance of power – Britain's traditional concern – and not in defence of Poland's independence, whatever the parliamentary rhetoric may have suggested otherwise. There was no British undertaking to restore Poland's eastern border, particularly as the one imposed by Stalin substantially corresponded to the Curzon Line advocated by Britain at the Paris Peace Conference in 1919. Accordingly, Britain's declaration of war the moment Germany invaded Poland was motivated primarily by her own interests and not those of Poland. From 1940 onwards Churchill's priority, backed by the United States, was to hold together the anti-German alliance, even if that entailed sacrificing vital Polish interests in deference to Stalin or anyone else. It follows, therefore, that although Sikorski was constrained by his government's financial and diplomatic dependence on Britain, he was naive and foolish in placing as much faith in Churchill as he did – an attitude which was curiously analogous to that of American President Franklin Roosevelt towards Stalin.[50]

It is in the context of these significant weaknesses and pressures that Sikorski's performance as leader of the Government-in-Exile has to be assessed, while at the same time paying due heed to his errors and misjudgements. The overall picture to emerge is that although he deserves much credit for reorganizing the widely dispersed Polish forces into a significant component of the Allied war effort, beginning with the part played by Polish airmen in the Battle of Britain in 1940, and including the resistance movement in Poland itself (*Armia Krajowa*),[51] most other major initiatives launched during his premiership ended in failure, most notably his policy towards the Soviet Union.

It appears that in November 1939, barely a few weeks after the Soviet occupation of Eastern Poland, Sikorski began to doubt whether that area could ever be fully recovered. Sometime later he concluded that at best the districts around Wilno and Lwów might be salvaged. But as the tide of international diplomacy turned against Poland, by 1943 he came to accept that this hope had also to be renounced. In the interim Sikorski developed the idea of Poland receiving compensation for the eastern territories at the expense of Germany.[52] It was not until his last visit to the United States in December 1942, however, that he presented to Roosevelt a memorandum detailing his thoughts on a post-war Polish–German border along the Oder-Neisse rivers. This arrangement was to form an integral part of a general shift in Poland's place in international affairs following the end of the war, based on reconciliation with the Soviet Union. As already noted, his attitude towards the Soviets had been far more flexible and positive than that adopted by the Polish government before 1939, if only because he perceived the need for Poland to enlist their support to counterbalance the primary threat from Germany. In other words, he wished to abandon the traditional Polish doctrine of 'two enemies' in favour of a policy which he believed was a more realistic reflection of Poland's geopolitical situation. It implied an acknowledgement that Poland was not the great power she had always claimed to be, but rather was a medium-sized state flanked by two infinitely stronger and antagonistic neighbours. However, Sikorski's enunciation of these ideas left much to be desired in terms of presentation, clarity and consistency, and consequently caused deep-seated and enduring resentment among his own cabinet and an overwhelming majority of the émigré community in Britain.

With Churchill exerting increasing pressure, Sikorski finally brought to fruition his aim of reaching an accommodation with the Soviet Union shortly after Germany launched 'Operation Barbarossa' in June 1941. The Soviet–Polish Pact of 30 July 1941 brought a number of benefits to the Poles, including the resumption of diplomatic ties and recognition of the Government-in-Exile, the release from captivity of tens of thousands of Poles captured in 1939 and a somewhat imprecise agreement to establish a Polish army in the USSR. On the other hand, there was no recognition or undertaking by the Soviets concerning the status of Poland's pre-war eastern provinces.[53] This was deemed unacceptable by some members of Sikorski's cabinet, and led to the resignations of Foreign Minister August Zalewski, the Minister in charge of Resistance, General Kazimierz Sosnkowski, and Marian Seyda, the Minister of Justice. They accused their leader of being too conciliatory towards Stalin, arguing with some justification that he could have secured better terms at a time when the Soviets were in a vulnerable position because of the Germans' sweeping victories against them.[54]

The pact never functioned satisfactorily. Disputes soon arose over the creation of the Polish army, the citizenship of Poles from the eastern areas of Poland annexed in 1939 and, not least, the fate of thousands of Polish officers captured by the Red Army in 1939. Above all, it was undermined by the failure to resolve the question of Poland's eastern border with the Soviet Union. Sikorski was probably at fault for not responding, for reasons which are not entirely clear, to Stalin's offer in December 1941 to negotiate a settlement of this intractable problem. At that moment the German advance was nearing Moscow. However, once the tide of war had turned in his favour as a result of the Soviet triumphs at Stalingrad and Kursk in 1943, Stalin was able to impose his will on relations with the Poles, who found no support from the British and Americans. They were desperately anxious to keep the Soviets in the Grand Alliance and to maintain a friendly basis for post-war cooperation.[55] Poland was effectively crushed in the middle. Stalin pressed home his advantage in April 1943, when he severed diplomatic relations with the Poles over the Katyń Affair, the discovery near Smolensk of the mass graves of thousands of Polish officers captured by the Soviets in 1939. For their part, the Poles could hardly have continued to work with a regime capable of such barbarism, and were destined to languish in a diplomatic no-man's-land. Churchill and the British Foreign Office became more and more patronizing and bullying;[56] Sikorski's Soviet policy lay in ruins, and bitter recriminations were unavoidable. Stalin was now free to attain what he had wanted all along: a Communist Poland under Soviet control. The Tehran and Yalta Conferences merely completed the formalities, without Polish participation.

Another major failure for Sikorski was the collapse by 1942 of his ambitious plan for a post-war Central European Federation, built on a Polish–Czechoslovak axis and envisaged as a counter-weight to Germany and the Soviet Union. The Czechs lost interest once Stalin voiced his opposition, and that was also sufficient for the British to come out against it.[57] In any event, the plan was unrealistic because it was fraught with practical difficulties and evoked little enthusiasm among Poles, many of whom had neither forgotten nor forgiven Czechoslovakia's hostile conduct over Cieszyn in 1918–19 and during the Polish–Soviet War a year later.

By the time of his death Sikorski's government had been irrevocably marginalized by the Allies. Although Polish troops were to fight in various theatres with much courage and success until the end of the war, with the Second Corps under General Władysław Anders and the First Armoured Division under General Stanisław Maczek in particular playing an exemplary role, their country's fate had already been sealed long before. The loss of Sikorski was the *coup de grâce* for the Polish cause. It is very doubtful whether he could materially have altered the course of events which culminated in tragic defeat in victory. That his successor, Stanisław Mikołajczyk, lacked stature and political sagacity only served to accentuate the overall disaster to have befallen the Poles.

The circumstances in which Sikorski and his entourage died have never been satisfactorily explained. The accident report compiled by the British authorities has been shown to be flawed,[58] while the Poles were not permitted to conduct their own investigation.[59] Repeated attempts by British intelligence circles to highlight putative plots by Soviet agents in the Polish Army to assassinate Sikorski[60] amount almost certainly to a red herring. Consequently, Polish suspicions of sabotage, either by the Soviets or British intelligence, or by both acting in consort, for motives related to the politics of the Grand Alliance, will be dispelled only when all relevant evidence has been made available.[61] The archives of the Soviet secret police (NKVD/KGB) and/or of MI6 might well contain a definitive answer,

General Sikorski is assured of a distinguished place in the annals of modern Polish history. For his military contribution to the creation and consolidation of the Second Republic in the years up to 1920–21 he deservedly became a national hero, and much of his work as Prime Minister in 1922–23 and Minister of War in 1924–25 was of lasting importance to the state. He was a noble representative of that generation of Poles who overcame so many obstacles to make a success of Polish independence in the inter-war years by dint of a sense of duty, Christian values and unswerving patriotism. If Sikorski's role in the nation's political life during 1928–39 was far less noteworthy, he at least made his reputation during that period as an eminent military theorist with a vision of the future. The final phase of his career in the Second World War was disappointing, however, for reasons which had to do with his difficult personality and errors of judgement, and even more to do with insurmountable extraneous influences. He symbolized with dignity and forbearance the spirit of Polish resistance to Nazi and Soviet tyranny, but ultimately fell foul of the cruel machinations of Allied power politics. None the less, it is entirely appropriate that Sikorski's remains were disinterred from the Polish military cemetery in Newark, Nottinghamshire, and on 17 September 1993 finally laid to rest with full state honours alongside the élite of Polish history in the crypt of Wawel Castle, Kraków, in a Poland once more free and independent.[62] His memory in this country continues to be cherished by various Polish bodies, notably the Polish Institute and Sikorski Museum in London.

NOTES

1.　　Walentyna Korpalska, *Władysław Eugeniusz Sikorski, Biografia Polityczna* (Ossolineum, Wrocław, 1981), p. 19.
2.　　R. Wapiński, *Władysław Sikorski* (Wiedza Powszechna, Warsaw, 1978), pp. 11 ff.
3.　　W. Jędrzejewicz, *Piłsudski: A Life for Poland* (Hippocrene Books, New York, 1982), pp. 54–60.
4.　　H. Roos, *A History of Modern Poland* (Eyre & Spottiswoode, London, 1966), p. 16.
5.　　T. Komarnicki, *Rebirth of the Polish Republic: A Study in the Diplomatic History of Europe, 1914–1920* (Heinemann, London, 1957), pp. 108–15.

6. J. Rzepecki, 'Rozejście się Sikorskiego z Piłsudskim w świetle korespondencji Izy Moszczeńkiej z sierpnia 1915r.', in *Kwartalnik Historyczny*, 47 (1960), No. 3, pp. 728–39.

7. P. D. Stachura, 'Poland 1918–1939: An Historical Assessment', in *Themes of Modern Polish History*, ed. P. D. Stachura (The Polish Social & Educational Society, Glasgow, 1992), pp. 19–22. Good background coverage in *The Reconstruction of Poland, 1914–23*, ed. P. Latawski (Macmillan, London, 1992).

8. P. A. Szudek, 'Sikorski as a strategist and military writer', in *Sikorski: Soldier and Statesman*, ed. K. Sword (Orbis, London, 1990), pp. 75 ff., 85 ff.

9. Sikorski's own account of the 1920 campaign is in his *Nad Wisłą i Wkrą, Studium z polskorosyjskiej wojny 1920 roku* (Zakład Narodowy im. Ossolińskich, Lwów, 1928). Further details in N. Davies, *White Eagle, Red Star: The Polish–Soviet War, 1919–20* (Macdonald, London, 1972), pp. 188–225, 226–63; A. Zamoyski, *The Battle for the Marchlands* (Columbia UP, 1981), pp. 125–40, 163–80. The diplomatic context is outlined in P. S. Wandycz, *Soviet–Polish Relations 1917–1921* (Harvard UP, 1969).

10. N. Davies, *God's Playground: A History of Poland, Vol. II. 1795 to the Present* (OUP, 1981), pp. 271, 419.

11. A. Polonsky, *Politics in Independent Poland 1921–1939* (OUP, 1972), *passim*.

12. W. Sikorski, *Polska Polityka Państwowa. Mowy i Deklaracje* (Zakł. Krakowkiej, Kraków, 1923), pp. 23 f., 41–2, 112–13, 127.

13. O. Terlecki, *Generał Ostatniej Legendy: Rzecz o Generale Władysławie Sikorskim* (Polonia, Chicago, 1976), p. 52.

14. F. Zweig, *Poland Between Two Wars: A Critical Study of Social and Economic Change* (Secker & Warburg, London, 1944), p. 36.

15. Jędrzejewicz, p. 175.

16. Terlecki, p. 52.

17. P. Korzec, *Juifs en Pologne. La question juive pendant l'entre-deux-guerres* (Univ. Presses, Paris, 1980), pp. 139–40; J. Marcus. *Social and Political History of the Jews in Poland, 1919–1939* (Mouton, New York, 1983), p. 307.

18. D. Engel, *In the Shadow of Auschwitz: The Polish Government-in-Exile and the Jews, 1939–1942* (Univ. of North Carolina Press, Chapel Hill, 1987), p. 233, n. 42.

19. E. Mendelsohn, *Zionism in Poland: The Formative Years, 1915–1926* (Yale UP, 1981), p. 219.

20. A. Garlicki, 'Relations between Sikorski and Pilsudski, 1907–28' in *Sikorski*, ed. Sword, pp. 40 f.

21. J. Rothschild, *Piłsudski's Coup d'Etat* (Columbia UP, New York, 1966), pp. 26 f.

22. A. Żółtowski, *Border of Europe: A Study of the Polish Eastern Provinces* (Hollis & Carter, London, 1950), p. 319.

23. Jędrzejewicz, pp. 196 ff., 210, 214–15.

24. *Ibid.*, p. 222.

25. Rothschild, pp. 47–154.
26. *Ibid.*, pp. 105 ff.; W. Sikorski, 'Kartki z dziennika', in *Żołnierz Polski*, 13 (July 1957), pp. 4 ff., and 14 (July 1957), pp. 14 f.
27. J. Rothschild, *East Central Europe between the Two World Wars* (University of Washington Press, Seattle, 1974), pp. 63 f.; the BBWR is the subject of A. Chojnowski, *Piłsudczycy u władzy. Dzieje Bezpartyjnego Bloku Współpracy z Rządem* (IHP, Warsaw, 1986).
28. W. Pobóg-Malinowski, *Najnowsza historia polityczna Polski, 1864–1945*, ii (Gryf. London, 1956), p. 460.
29. Szudek, in *Sikorski*, p. 91.
30. W. Sikorski, *Przyszła wojna. Jej możliwości i charakter oraz związane z nim zagadnienia obrony kraju* (Warsaw, 1934). The English version is entitled *Modern Warfare* (Hutchinson, London, 1942).
31. Terlecki, pp. 64–71; Wapiński, pp. 192–5.
32. Korpalska, pp. 159–60; Wapiński, pp. 182–3.
33. W. Sikorski, *Polska i Francja w przeszłości i dobie współczesnej* (Lwów, 1931).
34. Korpalska, pp. 189–90; S. Kot, *Listy z Rosji do Gen. Sikorskiego* (Jutro Polski, London, 1955), pp. 11–12: 'General Sikorski's 1936–9 Diary (Extracts)', in *Polish Perspectives*, 13 (1970, May), pp. 26–42. Translated by E. Rothert.
35. M. Kukiel, *Generał Władysław Sikorski – żołnierz i mąż stanu Polski Walczącej* (Sikorski Historical Institute, London, 1970), ch. 4; Korpalska, p. 185.
36. A. Polonsky, 'Sikorski as Opposition Politician, 1928–35', in *Sikorski*, ed. Sword, p. 50.
37. Korpalska, pp. 179 ff.
38. H. Przybylski, *Front Morges w okresie II rzeczypospolitej* (Warsaw, 1972), pp. 52–3; E. D. Wynot, *Polish Politics in Transition: The Camp of National Unity and the Struggle for Power, 1935–1939* (University of Georgia Press, 1974), pp. 31 f, 46 f.
39. K. Popiel, *Generał Sikorski w mojej pamięci* (Odnowa, London, 1978), pp. 70–83.
40. On OZON, J. Majchrowski, *Silni, zwarci, gotowi, Myśl Polityczna Obózu* (Warsaw, 1985); A. Chojnowski, *Koncepcje polityki narodowościowej rządów polskich w latach 1931–1939* (Wrocław, 1979), esp. pp. 220 ff.; Wynot, *Camp of National Unity, passim.*
41. Sikorski, *Modern Warfare*, p. 176.
42. Engel, p. 231, n. 28.
43. Terlecki, pp. 234–7; Kukiel, p. 112.
44. M. Kridl, J. Wittlin and W. Malinowski, *The Democratic Heritage of Poland* (Allen & Unwin, London, 1944), pp. 193–4, 196–7.
45. *Ibid.*, pp. 196–7.
46. J. Retinger, *Memoirs of an Eminence Grise* (Sikorski Historical Institute, London, 1972), pp. 109–11. Sikorski's memorandum of 19 June 1940 on his government's policy towards the USSR is printed

in *Documents on Polish–Soviet Relations, 1939–45*, ed. Sikorski Historical Institute, i (Heinemann, London, 1961), nos. 76, 95.

47. The best-informed and most critical account of the British approach is given in S. Zochowski, *British Policy in Relation to Poland in the Second World War* (Vantage Press. New York, 1988). Contrast this with M. Kitchen, *British Policy Towards the Soviet Union during the Second World War* (Croom Helm, London, 1986), which reveals a consistent pro-Soviet bias. See also G. Kacewicz, *Great Britain, the Soviet Union, and the Polish Government in Exile, 1939–45* (The Hague, 1979).

48. Kay Lundgreen-Nielsen, *The Polish Problem at the Paris Peace Conference: A Study of the Policies of the Great Powers and the Poles, 1918–1919* (Odense UP, 1979), pp. 69–70.

49. S. Newman, *The British Guarantee to Poland, March 1939: A Study in the Continuity of British Foreign Policy* (OUP, 1976).

50. Further details in P. S. Wandycz, *The United States and Poland* (Harvard UP, 1980); R. Lukas, *The Strange Allies: The United States and Poland, 1941–45* (University of Tennessee Press, 1978); J. Karski, *The Great Powers and Poland 1919–1945. From Versailles to Yalta* (University Press of America, 1985).

51. The text of the Anglo-Polish Military Agreement of August 1940 is in *Polskie Siły Zbrojne w Drugiej Wojnie Światowej*, Vol. II, Part I (Sikorski Historical Institute, London, 1959), pp. 226–30; J. Garliński, *Poland in the Second World War* (Macmillan, London, 1985), pp. 87–92, 120–38.

52. Sarah Meiklejohn Terry, *Poland's Place in Europe: General Sikorski and the Origin of the Oder–Neisse Line, 1939–1943* (Princeton UP, 1983), esp. pp. 38–65, 175–83.

53. The text of the treaty is in *Documents on Polish–Soviet Relations, op. cit.*, pp. 108–14.

54. *The Great Powers and the Polish Question, 1941–1945*, ed. A. Polonsky (Orbis, London, 1976), pp. 18–19. A recent analysis of his Soviet policy concludes that it 'best served Polish national interests at the time'. See A. M. Cienciala, 'General Sikorski and the Conclusion of the Polish–Soviet Agreement of July 30, 1941: A Ressessment', *The Polish Review*, 41 (1996), No. 4, pp. 401–34.

55. A. Polonsky, 'Stalin and the Poles 1941–47', in *European History Quarterly*, 17 (1987), No. 4, pp. 453–92; A. Krzemiński, *Polen im 20. Jahrhundert. Ein historischer Essay* (Beck, Munich, 1993), p. 94.

56. *The Crime of Katyń: Facts and Documents*, ed. Polish Cultural Foundation (Caldra House, London, 1965); W. S. Churchill, *The Second World War*, iv (London, 1951), pp. 679–82.

57. Meiklejohn Terry, pp. 66–118, 315–34; P. S. Wandycz, *Czechoslovak–Polish Confederation and the Great Powers, 1940–1943* (Indiana UP, Bloomington, 1956).

58. D. Baliszewski, in *PLUS MINUS* magazine, 153 (Warsaw, 3–4 July 1993).

59. J. Bartelski, 'What Did Happen to General Sikorski?' in *Aeroplane Monthly* (September 1993), pp. 12–15.
60. See letter page in *The Times*, 5 July 1993.
61. For an introduction, see D. Irving, *Accident: The Death of General Sikorski* (Kimber, London, 1967); W. T. Kowalski, *Tragedia w Gibraltarze* (Krajowa Agencja Wydawnicza, Warsaw, 1982).

My thanks to Lieut. Col. P. A. Szudek for his informed views on the circumstances of Sikorski's death and also for a number of valuable references (private correspondence, June–September 1993).
62. Report in *The Times*, 18 September 1993.

5 General Stanisław Maczek: A Biographical Profile

In the modern era, from the seventeenth to the twentieth century, Poland has produced very few distinguished political personalities, but a host of military heroes. Other than Roman Dmowski, the National Democratic leader and ideologue, and most recently Lech Wałęsa, in his role as leader of *Solidarność*, the political sphere has been populated by, at best, competent worthies, and at worst by the grey-faced apparatchiks of the postwar Communist era. That military men have been pre-eminent may simply be a reflection of the peculiar nature of Poland's history, in which the struggle to preserve, regain and consolidate her freedom and independence has overriden everything else.

King Jan Sobieski III, the victor at Vienna in 1683 against the Turks, was arguably the first in a subsequent long line of Poles who achieved greatness on behalf of their country's interests on the battlefield. Among others, Tadeusz Kościuszko for his leadership of the Polish insurrection against the Russians in the early 1790s, Józef Piłsudski for his creation of the Polish Legions in 1914 and his stunning defeat of the Bolsheviks in the Polish–Soviet War of 1919–20, General Władysław Sikorski, a brilliant commander in that war and later Commander-in-Chief and political leader of the Polish Government-in-Exile from 1939 until his death four years later, and General Władysław Anders, who triumphed at Monte Cassino in 1944, spring readily to mind. For the different generations of the large Polish community in Scotland, however, a special place in this pantheon is reserved for General Stanisław Maczek, Commander of the First Polish Armoured Division from its establishment in Scotland in 1942 until the end of the Second World War. His fame does not lie only in his outstanding military exploits; he also came to personify from the earliest post-war years until his death in 1994 the indomitable

courage and patriotic spirit of the Free Poland that was sacri-
ficed on the altar of political and diplomatic expediency at the
Allied conferences at Tehran in December 1943 and at Yalta in
February 1945.

Stanisław Władysław Maczek was born into a middle-class,
Catholic family on 31 March 1892 in the small town of Szczerzec
in Galicia, then part of the Austro-Hungarian Empire, but later
situated in the south-eastern corner of the Second Polish Republic:
after 1945 and until the early 1990s it was incorporated into
the Soviet Union, and since then has been in the independent
Republic of the Ukraine. The nearest city was Lwów, then the
leading cultural centre of partitioned Poland to which he had a
lifetime attachment. His twin brother, Franciszek, was killed in
the First World War, in 1915, and his two younger brothers also
died in action: Karol in 1914, and Jan in the Polish–Soviet War in
1920. Maczek's father, Witold, a retired judge, had small solicitor's chambers in the nearby town of Drohobycz, which had a
substantial Jewish population and which developed as a main
centre of Poland's oil industry. He attended secondary school
there, where one of his best friends was Bruno Schulz, a victim
of a Gestapo shooting in the German-occupied town in November
1942, but better recalled as an outstanding Jewish writer and fan-
tasist.[1] Although there was a Croatian element in the distant family background,[2] the young, somewhat studious Maczek grew up
in a wholesomely patriotic Polish household, though a military
career was never envisaged for him.

Indeed, from 1910 until the outbreak of the First World War he
studied philosophy and Polish philology at the Jan Kazimierz
University in Lwów, and also found time to become involved
in the Riflemen's Association, a paramilitary group headed by
Józef Piłsudski, who was preparing the ground for a fully fledged
Polish Army that would be ready to fight for Poland's independence when the opportunity arose. Then, a few months before
graduation, he was called up when the war began to the Austro-
Hungarian Army, serving in the crack II Kaiser Jaeger Regiment
(High Mountain and Ski Detachment) on the Italian front virtually until the end of the conflict.[3] During a three-month break in
the winter of 1917/18 to convalesce from wounds, he completed

his university diploma, returning to the front in summer 1918. Maczek was already shaping up as a good soldier. His bravery, strong character and ruggedness commended him to his superiors, and, finishing with the rank of *Oberleutnant*, he was awarded a number of Austrian decorations, including the Bronze Medal for Valour.[4]

Shortly after the end of the war and defeat for the Habsburgs, Maczek returned home and joined the nascent Polish Army. In the following few years, as Poland was engaged on a number of fronts to secure her frontiers that had not been determined by the Paris Peace Conference, he found himself in the thick of the fighting, firstly as commander of the Krosno Company for the liberation of Lwów from the Austrian-backed Ukrainian nationalist forces, and subsequently in successful battles for other parts of Eastern Galicia, notably Drohobycz, Borysław, Kałusz and Stanisławów.[5] During these last encounters of the Polish–Ukrainian War of 1918–19 Maczek was promoted to Captain on the battlefield by the Head of State and Commander-in-Chief, Piłsudski. There was no time to relax, however, as Poland was then threatened by the Red Army. Maczek took part in the Polish expedition in spring 1920 that culminated in the capture of Kiev, but soon found himself joining the retreat under pressure from a Bolshevik counter-offensive. That summer he organized and led the *Lotna* Mobile Assault Battalion of the First Cavalry Division, which saw action around Lwów against the notorious Red cavalry, the *Konarmiya*. He was admired for his adroit use of the *taczanka*, a heavy machine-gun mounted on a sprung cart, a prototype tank. The Poles' total defeat of the Soviet Bolsheviks following the victory at Warsaw ('Miracle on the Vistula') in August 1920 soon led to the successful conclusion of the struggle of the Second Republic to establish its borders, which were finally accorded international recognition in 1923.[6] Maczek earned promotion to Major.

Although Maczek had served his country well, his thoughts at the end of this turbulent period turned once more to academia. During his short break from the front in 1917/18 he had outlined a topic for a doctoral thesis and now, in autumn 1920, he looked forward to resuming his university studies. However, his military superiors, recognizing his many martial qualities, persuaded him to make the army his career. As was to be revealed in due course, it was a momentous decision, for both himself and Poland. Over the next few decades, Maczek progressed through the higher echelons of the army, assuming posts of increasing importance and attracting awards, thus giving a lie to the often-expressed view that those from a background in the Austrian-Hungarian Army found difficulty in advancing in a post-war Polish Army based largely on the Piłsudskiite tradition and personnel. In 1924 Maczek graduated as one of the top students of his year from the General Staff College in Warsaw, then headed the Intelligence Station in Lwów for three years, and from 1929 until 1935 commanded, as Colonel from 1931, the 81st Infantry Regiment in Grodno, in north-eastern Poland.

These were happy and fulfilling years for him, in a rejuvenated Poland which was making great strides despite formidable obstacles in many important areas of development, and in which the Army, especially the officer corps, basked in high social esteem as a result of its victorious defence of the national interest in the early 1920s. Colonel Maczek, who had married the lovely and vivacious Zofia Kuryś in June 1928, epitomized the outstanding personal qualities of a senior Polish Army officer of that era: he combined, in the highest order, toughness, courage, idealism, integrity and strength of character with the inimitable sense of honour and civility of an educated Polish gentleman. Overarching these supreme qualities was a passionate commitment to patriotic values. He was highly regarded by Piłsudski, and formed part of the guard of honour on the Marshal's death in May 1935.[7]

In 1935 Colonel Maczek was appointed Deputy Commander of the 7th Infantry Division at Częstochowa and continued to collect awards for his outstanding work, including the Gold Cross of Merit, the Hungarian Cross of Merit and the Order of the Romanian Crown. His interest in and promotion of ideas of mobile armoured warfare since 1918 led in October 1938 to his most significant appointment to date, that of Commander of the 10th Motorized Cavalry Brigade, Poland's first armoured tactical formation, whose worth had not yet been accepted by the Army

High Command. Maczek led the unit of some 5,000 men during the international crisis over Czechoslovakia, which resulted in the disputed area of Cieszyn being recovered by Poland in October 1938. The aggressively expansionist foreign policy being pursued by Nazi Germany relentlessly moved on to other parts during the following year, with Poland coming under more and more threat as she defied Hitler's pressure in the expectation that, in the event of war, she would have the support of her long-standing ally, France, and of her recent ally, Britain.[8] No-one had anticipated the Hitler–Stalin Pact in August 1939, which was aimed at destroying Poland as an independent state and partitioning her for a fourth time.

Despite the heroic, unaided resistance of the Polish Armed Forces against the invading *Wehrmacht* in the September Campaign in 1939, the Second Republic was defeated. Maczek's 10th Cavalry Brigade had been ordered west of Kraków in August to form part of Army 'Kraków', defending Silesia and the southern border area. Soon his unit was fighting hard to delay the advance of the XXII German Panzer Corps through southern Poland, but, caught by the Soviet invasion from the East in mid-September, it was ordered by the Polish General Staff to cross into Hungary on 19 September, which it did, in textbook fashion, fully armed and with regimental colours proudly held aloft.[9] None the less, the Brigade had earned the respect for its fighting qualities of its German opponents, who named it the 'Black Brigade' after the Commander's black leather coat.[10] In commemoration of this unusual accolade the unit's uniform henceforth bore a black left shoulder strap, consciously worn as the mark of an élite outfit.[11]

Along with other remnants of the Polish Army, Maczek and his men were interned in Hungary. Characteristically, however, they escaped, and before long were arriving in France, ready and anxious to continue the fight. In October 1939 General Władysław Sikorski, the newly appointed Prime Minister of the Polish Government-in-Exile, and shortly to be named also Commander-in-Chief of the Polish Armed Forces, promoted Maczek to Major-General and awarded him the Gold Cross of the most coveted Polish military decoration, the *Virtuti Militari*, in recognition of his unit's performance against the Germans. His partly reformed and under-equipped unit, the 10th Armoured Cavalry Brigade, based at Coëtquidan in Brittany, participated courageously in the disastrous French campaign of 1940, managing to defeat a German armoured brigade on the day the armistice was signed. It was then ordered to disperse and regroup in southern France, and from there the men were to make their way to Britain.[12]

Maczek engineered his escape in disguise via Marseilles to North Africa, and after a series of strange adventures in Morocco and Portugal, reached Casablanca, where, miraculously, he met up with his wife and two young children, Renata and Andrzej. With the aid of the Polish Military Attaché in Lisbon, the family found places on a plane to Bristol, landing on 21 September 1940. Thousands of Polish soldiers had already gathered in Scotland, and when Maczek arrived there himself his primary aim was to rebuild his armoured unit. In the mean time he and his men, now veterans of armoured warfare, were given, somewhat incongruously, the task of guarding the east coast of Scotland between Carnoustie and Montrose against a possible German invasion. Whatever may have been developing in the Whitehall corridors of power, life in exile during these early war years was made very pleasant for the Poles by the warm and sympathetic response of the Scottish people, who regarded them as gallant allies.[13] Quartered in various camps around the country, their dash, good manners and chivalry were widely appreciated, particularly by Scottish women, and the fact that most of them were practising Catholics did not seem to matter, at least for the time being, in a country which in parts was traditionally scarred by religious sectarianism.

Maczek's determination to re-establish his men as an armoured formation finally paid off in February 1942, when General Sikorski appointed him to lead the newly formed First Polish Armoured Division. A long period of intensive training followed, mainly in the Scottish borders around the small, picturesque town of Duns, which, many years later, on the occasion of Maczek's 100th birthday, made him a Freeman of the town in recognition of the wartime achievements of his unit. Undergoing intensive training, closely supervised by Maczek, the division was soon warmly praised by his superiors, including General Dwight D. Eisenhower, the Supreme Allied Commander, and Field Marshal Sir Bernard Montgomery, for its high level of discipline, smart appearance, panache and, above all, unique *esprit de corps*.[14] The strong bond of camaraderie uniting officers and men emanated directly from Maczek himself, for his personal charm and solicitude for his men permeated all activity. They, in turn, reciprocated by devising for him the sobriquet *Baca*, meaning 'Chief Shepherd', as a token of their trust, affection and esteem. Eventually, after almost four years of waiting and preparing in the wings, the moment Maczek had been counting on finally arrived, when his division joined the Allied invasion of Normandy.

On 1 August 1944, the day that the Warsaw Rising by the Home Army began, the 13,000-strong division, which was part of the Second Canadian Corps, landed on the beaches at Arromanches in what it hoped would be the first step of a campaign leading all the way to Warsaw. It was immediately involved in the thick of battle.[15] In mid-August, against fierce opposition from a German 7th Army that included the fanatical 12th SS Panzer Division *Hitlerjugend* under Kurt Meyer,[16] Maczek's men closed the Falaise Gap at Chambois, a pivotal turning-point in the entire Normandy campaign, as Montgomery later admitted.[17] Maczek's tactical skill, clear vision and uncanny talent for acting decisively at the most propitious moment coalesced with the bravery of his soldiers to assure victory. Thereafter, the division swept aside further stiff German resistance, playing an instrumental role in the liberation of towns across Northern France, including Abbeville and St Omer, before crossing into the Low Countries, where Ypres, Passchendaele, Ghent and Breda were among the towns to welcome the all-conquering Poles in October 1944.[18] Breda in particular was of special significance to Maczek and his troops, for the townspeople were eternally grateful that their freedom had been achieved by a manoeuvre by them which had spared the historic Old Town. That gratitude was most poignantly expressed by the conferment of honorary citizenship on General Maczek and his division.[19] A large cemetery there for the Poles who gave their lives in the campaign continues to this day to be well cared for by the town. On his death Maczek was also buried there, alongside his devoted soldiers. In many other towns and villages across northern France, Holland and Belgium, the division and its commander are still revered, with numerous streets, squares, monuments and other buildings named after them.

After a brief period of replenishment and reorganization, the division pushed on, crossing into Germany at the beginning of 1945, and freeing Polish women who, captured during the Warsaw Rising, had been interned in Stalag VI C at Oberlangen. In early May 1945 the division was delighted to accept the German surrender at Wilhelmshaven, the headquarters of German Naval Command, over which the Polish flag was hoisted. It was a supremely satisfying moment, reversing the outcome of six years previously. For the division, the closing stages of the war had been one long string of outstanding victories, enabling Maczek to emerge as one of the most successful and highly decorated of all the Allied military leaders. Indeed, he had maintained the astonishing record of never having lost a single battle since 1939. Following the unconditional surrender of the Third Reich, the First Armoured Division took up administrative duties in the North German town of Haren, which was promptly renamed 'Maczków' as a tribute to the General. Military analysts are agreed that the division was one of the finest fighting units of the war, and that Maczek was one of the most accomplished commanders.[20]

General Maczek did not remain in Germany for long, for in late May 1945 he was appointed Commanding Officer of the First Polish Corps, with headquarters in Scotland, and was promoted to Lieutenant-General. From December 1945 he was also General Commanding Officer of Polish Forces in the United Kingdom, where his principal responsibility ways to facilitate the demobilization of the Polish soldiers through the British-government-sponsored Polish Resettlement Corps.[21] Maczek himself was demobbed, at the age of only 56 and at the height of his professional powers, on 9 September 1948. For him, his troops and the cause of a Free Poland for which they had fought so courageously and triumphantly alongside the British, Americans and other Allied forces,[22] the Second World War had ended, thanks to cynical, pusillanimous decisions taken finally at the Yalta Conference, in humiliating political defeat despite brilliant military victory.[23]

Poland had been sold out to the Soviet Union, which was allowed to annex with impunity over 40 per cent of the territory of the pre-war Polish Republic and to install a puppet Communist regime in Warsaw, one of whose first spiteful acts was to strip Maczek of his Polish citizenship.[24] His numerous further decorations, including, from Britain, the Distinguished Service Cross and Companion of the Order of the Bath, from Holland the Order of Orange-Nassau, from France the *Legion d'Honneur* (Commander) and *Croix de Guerre avec Palme*, and from Belgium the *Ordre de la Couronne avec Palme*, were little consolation for a patriotic Pole amidst such overwhelming, undeserved tragedy. He never set foot again in his beloved Poland. A new, uncertain life of exile beckoned for him and his men, the vast majority of whom refused to return to a Soviet-dominated Communist Poland, the very antithesis of what they had fought for.

Settling in Edinburgh with his family, now with the addition of a second daughter, Magda, who was born in Scotland, General Maczek worked for a number of years in various jobs, including bartending in a hotel owned by one of his former soldiers, before retiring in 1965. None of these posts did justice, of course, to his eminent stature. That appropriate employment, such as lecturing in a staff college, was not found for him by the British authorities was an unqualified disgrace which continues to rankle with his countless admirers. This most honourable and dignified of men politely but firmly rejected several attempts by his former soldiers and others to raise funds on his behalf. Instead, with the unstinting support of his wife, he worked tirelessly for the wounded and disabled Polish ex-servicemen in Edinburgh. His modest lifestyle, which included hill-climbing and fishing as recreations, did not prevent him, however, from emerging as the natural if unofficial leader of the substantial exiled Polish community scattered throughout Scotland,[25] and his men at home and abroad continued to honour him through their Divisional Association. In his memoirs, he typically understated his own role in a military career that spanned over thirty years, while making generous acknowledgement of that of his 'Boys', as he liked to call them, the 'Old Guard of the Republic'.[26] Unlike another war hero, General Władysław Anders, he refused to become embroiled in the often bitter internecine disputes among the émigré community in London, and for that reason tended to be somewhat marginalized. Time has shown, however, that his was a wise decision and that it would have been to the advantage of the émigré community if others had followed his example.

General Maczek's uncompromising repudiation of the Polish Communist regime and its Soviet backers from 1945 until its ignominious disintegration in 1989/90 further endeared him to his fellow countrymen and to a second generation of Polish background in Scotland, whose traditionally patriotic values he inspirationally epitomized. For them all, he was the towering symbol of defiance and resistance to tyranny. Several attempts over the years by ministers and other officials of the Warsaw regime to establish contact with him, even as it was falling apart, were dismissed out of hand because he regarded them, quite rightly, as the illegitimate representatives of the country he had served with such unswerving devotion and distinction.[27] It was presumably for this reason that on his visit to Scotland in June 1982, the Pope is reputed to have greeted Maczek with the words, 'you are a slice of history'.[28] Happily, unlike many of his generation, he lived to witness the end of the sterile Communist interlude and the restoration of a free and independent Poland – for the second time this century.

The General's 100th birthday on 31 March 1992 was the occasion for an impressive celebration spanning several continents, somewhat to the surprise of this modest, unassuming personality, whose health had finally begun to decline. Warm messages of congratulation came from many international dignitaries, including from his countryman, Pope John Paul II, the Queen, President Lech Wałęsa, President George Bush, President François Mitterrand, King Baudouin of Belgium and Queen Beatrice of the Netherlands, as well as from the Mayors of towns his division had liberated in the war. The town of Rzeszów, in southern Poland, where the 10th Brigade had been raised, made him an Honorary Freeman. He was also promoted to full General by the post-Communist Polish government. An International Symposium dedicated to his life and career was organized by the Polish community in Glasgow, and a number of academic publications saluted a very special centenary, all evidence that he had attained that most elusive status, a veritable legend in his own lifetime.[29]

General Maczek died peacefully at home in Edinburgh on 11 December 1994, thus bringing to an end a particular era in the history of the Polish community in Scotland,[30] a fact underlined a few months later when his wife, affectionately and respectfully known as '*Pani Generałowa*', or 'Mrs General', also passed away.[31] Maczek's exemplary contribution to the Polish cause as an officer and patriot throughout his long and distinguished life is a source of pride and inspiration to the present and future generations of Poles. He will be forever remembered with the deepest affection, gratitude and admiration as one of the finest and most important figures in the history of modern Poland. This exalted status was officially recognized, in fact, on 16 February 1994, when he was invested by special decree of President Wałęsa with the coveted Order of the White Eagle (Knight Companion), which has been bestowed on only a handful of illustrious Poles this century. In a further, posthumous tribute, a memorial plaque in his honour was unveiled by the Lord Provost of Edinburgh at the General's former home in the city on 11 December 1997, the third anniversary of his death.[32] All told, General Maczek is, incontrovertibly, the quintessential Polish hero.

NOTES

1. Schulz, a Polish-speaking Jew, was born in the same year as Maczek, in Drohobycz, where he became an art teacher. He wrote short stories recalling a traditional Jewish world in the town which had already faded before 1939. These stories are published in his *The Streets of Crocodiles* (McGibbon & Kee, London, 1963). Another volume is his *Sanatorium under the Sign of the Hourglass* (Hamish Hamilton, London, 1979). Further information on Schulz's work in Edward Rogerson, 'Images of Jewish Poland in the Post-War Polish Cinema', *Polin*, 2 (1987), pp. 359–71; J. Ficowski (ed.), *Letters and Drawings of Bruno Schulz, with Selected Prose* (Harper & Row, New York, 1988); and Henri Lewi, *Bruno Schulz* (London, 1989).
2. Information to the author from Dr Andrzej Maczek, the General's son, 7 December 1997.

3.   These battles on the Isonzo River above Trieste are graphically described in Ernest Hemingway's novel *A Farewell to Arms*.

4.   Andrzej Suchcitz, 'Generał Stanisław Maczek', in Juliusz L. Englert and Krzysztof Barbarski, *Generał Maczek. I Żołnierze 1 Dywizji Pancernej* (Polish Cultural Foundation, London, 1992), p. 8.

5.   Stanisław Maczek, *Od Podwody Do Czołga. Wspomnienia Wojenne 1918–1945* (Orbis, London, 1961), pp. 15–47.

6.   Peter D. Stachura, 'The Battle of Warsaw, August 1920, and the Development of the Second Polish Republic', in Peter D. Stachura (ed.), *Poland Between the Wars, 1918–1939* (Macmillan, London, 1998).

7.   Englert and Barbarski, *Maczek*, p. 28.

8.   Background details in Simon Newman, *March 1939: The British Guarantee to Poland* (Clarendon Press, Oxford, 1976); Piotr S. Wandycz, *France and Her Eastern Allies, 1919–1925* (University of Minnesota Press, Minneapolis, 1962), and *idem, The Twilight of French Eastern Alliances, 1926–1936* (Princeton University Press, Princeton, NJ, 1988).

9.   Maczek, *Od Podwody Do Czołga*, pp. 74–99.

10.   Maczek's famous coat was the centrepiece of an outstanding exhibition organized at the Scottish United Services Museum, Edinburgh Castle, 1993–96, on the theme 'For Your Freedom And Ours: Poland, Scotland and the Second World War'. An eponymous brochure by Allan Carswell is available (National Museums of Scotland, Edinburgh, 1993).

11.   Witold A. Deimel, 'The Life and Career of General Stanisław Maczek: An Appreciation', in Peter D. Stachura (ed.), *Themes of Modern Polish History* (The Polish Social and Educational Society, Glasgow, 1992), p. 11.

12.   Suchcitz, in Englert and Barbarski, *Maczek*, p. 10.

13.   Allan L. Carswell, 'Gallant Allies – The Early Years of the Polish Military Presence in Scotland, 1940–42', paper delivered to a meeting of The Polish Society at the University of Glasgow, 24 February 1998.

14.   Eisenhower's letter of appreciation of 17 April 1944 to Maczek is reproduced in Englert and Barbarski, *Maczek*, p. 140. It was during Montgomery's inspection of the division on 13 March 1944 that he made the infamous remark to Maczek: 'What language do the Poles use among themselves, German or Russian?' The General's reply is not recorded.

15.   The best account of the division's part in the campaign is by P. A. Szudek, 'The First Polish Armoured Division in the Second World War', in Stachura (ed.), *Themes*, pp. 33–64. A broader view is in John Keegan, *Six Armies in Normandy* (Penguin, London, 1982).

16.   See Kurt Meyer, *Grenadiere* (Munich, 1956). The German 7th Army was commanded by Field Marshal Günther von Kluge.

17.   Szudek in Stachura (ed.), *Themes*, pp. 42–53.

18.   Maczek, *Od Podwody Do Czołga*, pp. 148–216.

19. The letters of award are reproduced in Englert and Barbarski, *Maczek*, pp. 36, 149.

20. Szudek in Stachura (ed.), *Themes*, p. 57.

21. Keith Sword, with Norman Davies and Jan Ciechanowski, *The Formation of the Polish Community in Great Britain, 1939–1950* (School of Slavonic and East European Studies, London, 1989), pp. 245–55. See also Peter D. Stachura, 'The Polish Minority in Scotland: 1945 until the Present', in this volume.

22. There are good summaries of the Polish military effort in Andrzej Suchcitz, *Poland's Contribution to the Allied Victory in the Second World War* (Polish Ex-Combatants' Association, London, 1995), and Tadeusz Modelski, *The Polish Contribution to the Ultimate Allied Victory in the Second World War* (privately published, Worthing, 1986).

23. The Polish Government-in-Exile, *The Yalta Agreements: Documents prior to, during and after the Crimea Conference 1945*, Ed. Zygmunt C. Szkopiak (London, 1986). The background is usefully conveyed in Sikorski Historical Institute, *Documents on Polish–Soviet Relations, 1939–1945* (Heinemann, London, 1961), and Stanisław Mikołajczyk, *The Rape of Poland: The Pattern of Soviet Aggression* (Whittlesey House, New York, 1948).

24. Information from Dr Andrzej Maczek, 7 December 1997.

25. Tomasz Ziarski-Kernberg, *The Polish Community in Scotland* (doctoral thesis, University of Glasgow, 1990) has collated some useful factual data from official records.

26. Maczek, *Od Podwody Do Czołga*, which makes no comment on the post-1945 period.

27. The latest attempt was made in March 1989 by the Polish Prime Minister, Mieczysław Rakowski, who apologised to the General for the treatment he had received from the Warsaw regime and invited him to return to Poland. Rakowski's letter was returned to the Polish Consulate in Edinburgh without acknowledgement.

28. Information from private sources.

29. These details are from Peter D. Stachura, 'Report. Themes of Modern Polish History. An International Symposium', *Scottish Slavonic Review*, 18 (1992), pp. 145–8. See also *idem* (ed.), *Themes of Modern Polish History: Proceedings of a Symposium on 28 March 1992 in Honour of the Centenary of General Stanisław Maczek* (The Polish Social and Educational Society, Glasgow, 1992), and Englert and Barbarski, *Maczek, op. cit.* Maczek was the only Honorary Member of the latter society.

30. Obituries by Adam Zamoyski in *The Independent*, 13 December 1994, *The Times*, 13 December 1994 (anonymous), and Peter D. Stachura in *The Scotsman*, 12 December 1994. A special edition of *Pancerniak*, the organ of the First Polish Armoured Division Association, 27 (1995), No. 53, was also devoted to the General, whose private papers are now in the archives of the Polish Institute and Sikorski Museum, London.

31.   Obituary of Mrs Maczek in *The Scotsman*, 27 May 1995, by Irene
       Thornton and Peter D. Stachura.
32.   This was the third time that this signal honour had been bestowed on
       distinguished Poles with connections to Edinburgh. Frederick Chopin
       and Ignacy Paderewski were the other recipients.

6 Poles and Jews in the Second World War

The acrimonious debate concerning the role of Poles in the Holocaust relates not only to the question of anti-Semitism in the Second Republic before the outbreak of the Second World War, but also to relations between two persecuted groups under German and Soviet occupation. In addition to accusations that pre-war Polish anti-Semitism helped pave the way for the Holocaust, and that there was a degree of active Polish complicity in the extermination of Jews, the masses of ordinary Poles have been vilified for allegedly standing aside in apathy while Jews were being rounded up and transported to the death camps.[1] Examples of individual or instititutional Polish help for Jews are dismissed as largely insignificant and ineffective.[2]

The debate, and especially the endeavour to substantiate the charges levelled at the Poles from Jewish spokesmen, has led to a searching analysis of a broad range of multifarious factors which shaped Poland's historical development since the regaining of independent statehood in 1918. At its most superficial and, it must be said, most unconvincing, critics have pointed to the fact that the Nazi extermination camps of Auschwitz, Treblinka, Sobibór, Majdanek and others were all located on Polish soil, as if this provides conclusive proof of Polish culpability. Fortunately, even some of Poland's fiercest accusers, such as Yisrael Gutman, have rejected this notion as untenable.[3] Of more relevance here was that over three million Jews were conveniently concentrated in a distant part of Eastern Europe under total Nazi control, and to which it made logistical sense to send Jews from across the rest of Europe to their death.

Until the late 1980s this historical controversy was conducted mainly by scholars living outside Poland, for during the period of Communist 'People's Poland' the topic, along with a number of others, notably the Nazi–Soviet Pact of 1939, the Soviet occupation of Eastern Poland from 1939 to 1941, the Katyń Massacre and the Yalta Agreement, was officially ignored, naturally, at the ultimate behest of the Soviet Union.[4] Contributions from, among others, Gutman, Krakowski, Mendelsohn and Ringelbaum went unchallenged as a result of political and ideological imperatives.[5] Rather crude, intermittent propaganda of an anti-Semitic flavour was about the sum total of the Communist regime's response. None the less, the rather sordid disagreement throughout the late 1970s and 1980s between the Warsaw regime and Jewish groups over the siting of a Carmelite convent at Auschwitz was but one public manifestation of ongoing tensions between Poles and Jews. Only following the intervention in more recent years of the Polish Pope, John Paul II, who has insisted on a series of friendly gestures and concessions towards the Jews, has this particular squabble subsided, though it continues to rumble on.[6]

Anti-Semitism had broken into the public domain for the first time in post-war Poland in 1967–8, when competing factions within the Communist Party employed it as part of a power struggle, and although popular interest in the Jewish past blossomed in the next decade, especially among younger Poles, it was the furore occasioned by the publication in early 1987 in the Kraków-based Catholic weekly '*Tygodnik Powszechny*' of Professor Jan Błonski's article, '*Biedni Polacy patrzą na getto*', that a response from scholars in Poland was forthcoming.[7] Błonski, who held the Chair of the History of Polish Literature at the Jagiellonian University in Kraków, was the first Polish academic to abandon an apologetic stance on this painful subject by sharply criticizing Polish attitudes towards the Jews in wartime Poland. His bold intercession had been encouraged by the well-known philose-mitic editor of the journal, Jerzy Turwicz, and since that moment discussion has broadened and intensified.

After denouncing the Catholic Church for sustaining antipathy towards Jews, 'thereby driving them into isolation and humiliation', Błonski continues with the accusation that Poles were guilty of an 'inadequate effort to resist' the Nazi treatment of the Jews, being at best indifferent to their fate. He argues further that pre-war Polish anti-Semitism facilitated the Holocaust. On these counts, therefore, he concurs with the principal arguments of the anti-Polish lobby. More sensationally, Błonski asserts, without adducing any evidence, that Poles would have actively assisted the Nazis in their grisly work, had not 'the hand of God' somehow restrained them. Once again, this is at one with a major point made by some historians, that there were numbers of Poles who did, after all, actively participate in the Holocaust by, for example, blackmailing and betraying Jews to the Gestapo, or even by shooting them outright. In the latter regard the extreme right-wing resistance organization, the National Armed Forces (NSZ), and sections of the main resistance movement, the Home Army (AK), are identified as having been particularly hostile towards the Jews (and Communists) in the closing stages of the war. It is an argument which really dresses some Poles in Nazi uniform. Błonski concludes his piece with the astonishing falsehood that 'it was nowhere else but in Poland, and especially in the twentieth century, that anti-Semitism became particularly virulent'.

The credibility of these statements and allegations against the wartime conduct of Poles towards the Jews is perhaps difficult to disentangle from the plethora of information and disinformation that has accumulated over the years. But having previously argued that the extent and importance of anti-Semitism in pre-war Poland have been grossly exaggerated, and matched in any case by Jewish polonophobia,[8] I consider that a review of the most pertinent developments in occupied Poland during the Second World War is demanded.

The tragic outcome of the September Campaign of 1939, despite the unaided heroism of the Polish Armed Forces, ushered in the darkest era in modern Polish history. The German invaders adopted from the beginning an occupation policy that was based on the most brutal racial ideology, at the core of which were anti-Semitism and slavophobia. From his earliest days as a political agitator, Adolf Hitler had made clear his almost pathological hatred of the Jews, whom he described in *Mein Kampf* as *Untermenschen*, or sub-humans, a cancer in German and European society which he was unshakeably resolved to remove.[9] Although racial anti-Semitism was a fundamental component of Nazi ideology and of the appeal he and his National Socialist Party (NSDAP) made during their rise to power before 1933, they had not publicly advocated the wholesale extermination of the Jews as their preferred method of addressing the 'Jewish problem'.[10] Once in power, the Nazi regime's policy towards the Jews in Germany steadily but inexorably intensified, from the aggressive boycotting of Jewish businesses in Spring 1933, the Nuremberg Race Laws in September 1935, the encouragement to emigrate, the destruction of Jewish property and synagogues in the so-called *Reichskristallnacht* ('Night of Broken Glass') in November 1938, to Hitler's declaration in the Reichstag the following year that a European war would result in the extinction of the Jewish race in Europe.[11] Confronted in 1939 by a substantial Jewish community in conquered Poland, the Nazis lost no time in introducing an organized programme of repression against both Jews and Poles which was the prelude to the mass slaughter of both.

The Nazi 'New Order' in Poland brought unparalleled terror, brutality and genocide to bear on all sections of the population.[12] By the end of it, and of the war itself, no fewer than 6 million Poles had been killed, half of them Jewish citizens of the Second Republic. Effective resistance to a totalitarian system such as that in the Third Reich was invariably impossible, and always highly dangerous, as exemplified by the marginal impact of the German anti-Nazi resistance movement from 1933 onwards.[13] The combination of the power of the German military, police and SS authorities, draconian laws and the ruthless implementation of an uncompromising racial ideology ensured that when the extermination of Jews was set in train in 1942 there was very little that the Poles could do to help them, except through small, individual acts of daring and compassion. According to a decree issued on 25 October 1941 by the German Governor, Hans Frank, helping Jews was punishable with the death penalty, and the Poles were further emasculated by the deportation of several million of the most able-bodied as slave labour to the Reich and the imposition of serf-like living conditions on the rest. Despite this, perhaps as many as 200,000 Jews were saved from extermination by the merciful intervention of Poles, 2,500 of whom were caught and executed for their trouble.[14]

What is perhaps remarkable, therefore, is that Poles actually found the time and resources to specifically consider the plight of the Jews in their midst. The clandestine Council for Aid to Jews (*Żegota*), which was set up in December 1942 by the Delegatura in Warsaw of the Polish government in London with branches in major cities, may have been limited by circumstances and resources in what could be achieved, but its very existence is a tribute to the many who gave it and the Polish Underground State that directed it on the ground their passive or active support.[15] This effort, unfortunately, was not reciprocated by the Jews, most of whom met their fate passively, as testified, for example, by the small and ineffectual underground resistance movement represented by ZOB (Jewish Combat Organizations) and the Jewish Military Union (ZZW). Indeed, some Jews, employed in the Jewish Councils (*Judenräte*) and Jewish Police (*Ordnerdienst*), actually made the control of their fellows easier in some ways for the Nazis. The Jewish Ghetto Rising in Warsaw in Spring 1943, however, was an honourable exception.[16] Furthermore, in view of the vicious anti-Polish behaviour of many Jews in Soviet-occupied Eastern Poland from 1939 until summer 1941, the courageous efforts made by Poles to help Jews thereafter is surely testimony to their unbroken sense of decency and humanity in the face of the most deadening barbarism.

The relatively few instances of Polish collaboration with the Nazis in hunting down Jews, as well as the murder of some Jews by the NSZ in 1944–5, are entirely unrepresentative of the wartime comportment of the Polish nation. It may well have been the case that the incessant anti-Semitic propaganda of the Nazis eventually left a mark on these aberrant elements of the Polish population, and some Polish underground newspapers and other publications did reflect this influence.[17] In other words, Poles of a radical right-wing or criminal disposition were possibly not entirely immune to hate-filled Nazi propaganda over a sustained period. Even so, the extent of Polish collaboration in denouncing and killing Jews was insignificant compared with the assistance given to the Germans in occupied France, Romania, the Baltic States and the Ukraine.[18] It is consequently a palpable untruth to claim that by 1943 'Polish Fascism and its ally, anti-semitism, have won over the majority of the Polish people'.[19] Nor was it the case, as several Jewish historians have alleged,[20] that the

Home Army waged a war against the small numbers of Jewish partisans under cover of opposing banditry in 1943–4. The Home Army, recognizing the growing scale of that problem in many parts of occupied Poland, took action against bandits regardless of nationality, so that of the 920 executions it carried out in 1943 and the first six months of 1944, most were of ethnic Poles, including some of its own members.[21]

More important to an understanding of the development of Polish–Jewish relations during the war, however, is the Jewish reaction to the Soviet invasion of Eastern Poland, beginning on 17 September 1939. It was welcomed in that area with 'estactic enthusiasm' by many of the large Jewish population, regardless of class or previous political affiliation,[22] and there were examples of military action by locally organized Jewish units in support of the Red Army, as had also been the case in 1920 during the Polish–Soviet War. An orgy of reprisal against ethnic Poles, especially estate owners, the professional classes and the military colonists who had arrived in the 1920s, was undertaken by Jews with the active collaboration of the Soviet Security Police (NKVD).[23] Murder, looting, confiscation and denunciation were soon to be followed by mass roundups of Poles in preparation for their expulsion into the remotest corners of the Soviet Union: over 1.5 million had been deported by summer 1941.[24] For these Eastern Jews the atrocities were sweet revenge for what they regarded, without justification, as their discriminatory treatment at the hands of Poles before the war, most recently in the course of the polonization drive in 1938–9 and the 'pacification' exercise of 1938. They openly rejoiced at the collapse of the Polish Republic, believing, erroneously as it soon transpired, that the day of national and class liberation had arrived. With their Soviet masters, they aimed at the effective depolonization of Eastern Poland.[25]

Only a small percentage of the Jewish community had been members of the Communist Party of Poland (KPP) during the inter-war era, though they had occupied an influential and conspicuous place in the party's leadership and in the rank and file in major centres, such as Warsaw, Łódź and Lwów. But a far greater number of younger Jews, often through the pro-Marxist *Bund*

(General Jewish Workers' Union) or some Zionist groups, had possessed an underlying sympathy for Communism and an affinity with Soviet Russia, both of which had been, of course, prime enemies of the Polish Second Republic. For these Jews Communism had an almost messianic appeal, while the Soviet Union was regarded as their natural homeland. As a result of these ideological, political and anti-Polish factors they found it easy after 1939 to join the Soviet bandwagon in Eastern Poland, and soon occupied prominent positions in industry, schools, local government, police and other Soviet-installed institutions. They went about their business with revolutionary zeal and an consuming hatred for all things Polish. As Soviet-Bolshevik commissars, they were the most fanatical.[26] Hence, the argument that their frenzied participation in the new Soviet administration was motivated by gratitude for being saved from the Nazis is patently unconvincing.[27] For their part, the Poles could not help but be bitterly aware of the Jews' attitudes and conduct, as Jan Karski vividly reported to the exiled Polish government in London,[28] and as General Stefan Grot-Rowecki, Commander of the Home Army, acknowledged in 1941.[29] It is certain that this adversely affected Polish attitudes towards the Jews until the end of the war and beyond. The radical-proletarian and pro-Communist pronouncements issued by the tiny Jewish underground resistance groups from time to time [30] hardly inspired confidence in a Polish population for whom extreme left-wing ideologies held little attraction before, during or after the war.

The type of behaviour and attitude displayed by many Jews in Eastern Poland between 1939 and 1941, when the Germans expelled the Soviets in the course of 'Operation Barbarossa', was linked by many Poles to other disasters that befell the Polish cause, notably the Katyń Massacre by the NKVD and Stalin's refusal in August 1944 to assist the Poles in the Warsaw Uprising. These actions were widely blamed on the nefarious machinations of 'Jewish Bolshevism'.

This is not to overlook the considerable efforts of General Władysław Sikorski's Polish government in London to immediately reassure the Jews, as part of a strategy that stressed its clean break with the pre-war *Sanacja* regime, that it was not anti-Semitic and that in a restored, independent Poland they would be treated on a fair and equitable basis, as declarations of 3 November 1940 and 10 December 1942 made explicit. In the latter, Jan Stańczyk, Minister of Labour and Social Welfare, announced: [31]

> Future relations between Gentiles and Jews in Liberated Poland will be built on entirely new foundations. Poland will guarantee all her citizens, including the Jews, full legal equality. Poland will be a true democracy, and every one of her citizens will enjoy equal rights, irrespective of race, creed or origin. ... Democratic Poland ... will give the Polish Jews ... a home.

The statement was warmly received by most Jewish leaders and organizations.[32]

Two Jews, Ignacy Schwarcbart and Szmul Zygielbojm, were brought into the advisory Polish National Council in London, and several occupied leading positions in the exiled government, including the former Polish Socialist Party stalwart, Herman Lieberman, who served until his death in 1941 as Minister of Justice, Henryk Strasburger as Treasury Minister, Adam Pragier as Minister of Information, and Ludwik Grosfeld as Minister of Finance (who returned to Poland after 1945 to join the Communist regime).[33] In the most trying of circumstances, particularly in the face of incessant complaints from Jewish representatives[34] at a time in 1941/2 when its political and diplomatic influence was beginning to seriously decline, the Polish government strove manfully to maintain good relations with the Jews. General Sikorski himself was not anti-Semitic and, for example, urged Poles to aid the Ghetto Rising in Warsaw, which some units of the Home Army undertook at great risk and cost in lives.

Sikorski's government also provided through its Delegatura in Warsaw increasingly generous financial support to the Council for Aid to Jews, funded stranded Polish Jews in France, paid for the transit of some Jews from Portugal to Britain, and facilitated the passage of large numbers of them from Europe to Latin America. Moreover, in April 1944 the Polish government established in London, in the face of Allied apathy and Jewish resignation, the Council for Rescuing Polish Jews, a well-intentioned if limited enterprise. Regrettably, however, these endeavours have been disparaged as unimportant and the Poles accused of acting from ulterior motives and self-interest.[35] At the same time the inevitable weaknesses, failures and omissions on the Polish side, including the absence of substantive contact between the Polish underground and the Jews in 1939–42,[36] and some evidence of anti-Semitism in the Polish army led out of the Soviet Union for the Middle East in 1942 by General Władysław Anders, have been unduly highlighted.[37] No matter what was done and what was not, this was always bound to be an extremely sensitive and delicate relationship. In any case, only the Allies had the resources to save the mass of Jews from extermination, but despite repeated exhortations from the Polish side from 1942 onwards, nothing was done.[38]

By the end of the war, Polish–Jewish relations were far worse than they had been at the beginning. Both communities had suffered immeasurably under the Nazis. The planned, systematic extermination of the Polish élites (the intelligentsia, landowners, clergy and army officers) and the slaughter of millions more was as heinous a crime as the mass extermination of the Jews in the gas chambers: the 'Forgotten Holocaust' of the Poles,[39] on the one hand, and the Holocaust of the Jews on the other. But other crucial events quickly increased distrust, suspicion and hatred on both sides.

In the first instance, the acquisition in 1945–6 by some Poles of former Jewish commercial and residential property, their jobs and material goods, and the use made of anti-Semitism by several right-wing political parties in their propaganda, undoubtedly soured relations further. The returning Jews were unwanted and resented for these reasons. Second, the rapacious nature of the Red Army's 'liberation' of Poland in 1944–5, beginning with its calculated failure to assist the Home Army-led Warsaw Uprising from August to October 1944, and continuing with its mass looting, deportations and killings (especially of Home Army personnel and other anti-Communists), convinced Poles that one totalitarian oppressor had simply been replaced by another. There was no question, therefore, of 'a democratic Polish Government ... [being] ... set up in a liberated Poland'.[40] The treacherous arrest and subsequent show trial in Moscow in June 1945 of the former commander of the Home Army, General Leopold Okulicki, the representative in Poland of the Polish

Government-in-Exile, and fourteen other prominent figures, was an especially instructive episode for the mass of Poles. The civil war that lasted until the late 1940s, involving Soviet-backed Communist forces, units of the nationalist resistance (principally, *Zrzeszenie Wolnośći i Niepodległośći*, the Freedom and Independence Group) and Ukrainian partisans, further embittered the atmosphere. By the end of the fighting, the organized anti-Communist military resistance had been permanently crushed.

Third, the Poles' acute feelings of disappointment and betrayal on learning of the outcome of the Yalta Conference in February 1945, by which, in line with decisions taken at the Tehran Conference in December 1943, the Allies agreed that over 40 per cent of the territory of the pre-war Republic, including the historic Polish cities of Lwów and Wilno, was to be annexed by the Soviet Union, underlined the heart breaking reality of their situation.[41]

Fourth, despite spurious talk of Soviet 'liberation' of Poland, a Communist government, totally alien to her traditions and subservient to the Soviet Union, was imposed. Bolshevism had finally triumphed, which for many Poles was synonymous with a 'Jewish victory'. The Western Allies' withdrawal of recognition in July 1945 of the Polish government in London, a faithful and brave ally during the entire war, was rightly seen as an act of the utmost cynicism, ingratitude and betrayal, complemented in January 1947 by the Communists' staging of transparently fraudulent elections without meaningful protest from the West.[42] Fifth, immediately following the end of the war a sizeable Jewish community began to reassemble in Poland, especially in Warsaw and several other cities. It lost no time in re-establishing its own press, theatre, publishing house, cooperatives, Historical Commission, social welfare network, political parties and even a Jewish section of the Communist Polish Workers Party (PPR). This activity was widely resented, particularly as many of these Jews were members of the pro-Communist intelligentsia and of the Communist party itself.[43]

Finally, and reinforcing the latter point, the incoming Soviet-controlled Communist regime had a comparatively large number of Jewish officials, especially in the hierarchy of the Polish Communist Party and the security services. Most of them, born and educated in Poland, had arrived from the Soviet Union in the wake of the Red Army's relentless advance along the Eastern Front. Invariably with assumed Polish names, they constituted an integral part of the new Red Establishment, emerging as the most dedicated proponents of a regime universally detested by Poles. Jakub Berman, the *éminence grise* of the new regime, enjoyed direct access to Stalin; others, such as Roman Zambrowski, Hilary Minc, Eugeniusz Szyr, Juliusz Katz-Suchy, Adam Schaff, Stefan Staszewski, Leon Kasman, Wiktor Grosz, Artur Starewicz, Jacek Rózański, Anatol Fejgin, Leon Szajn and Zygmunt Modzelewski, epitomized the formidable role of Jewish Communists in the Party, parliament, Army, secret police and security organs, the press and the ministries of Justice and Foreign Affairs. Polonophobia had been institutionalized with a vengeance by a Jewish Communist élite who remained in power until 1955/6.[44]

It is within a context shaped by these developments that anti-Semitism in Poland led, in the immediate aftermath of the Holocaust, to a outbreaks of violence. As a result of random violence 353 Jews were allegedly killed in 1945 alone, including pogroms in Rzeszów in July and in Kraków in August, though it may well be that most of these can be attributed to military rather than to ethnic clashes. In July 1946 the notorious pogrom in Kielce saw 42 Jewish deaths. The Holocaust, it seemed, was a Jewish affair of no wider relevance to Poles, who had their own tragedies to mourn, and they blamed the Jews for the greatest of them.[45] Paradoxically, therefore, anti-Semitism was stronger in Poland in the aftermath of the Holocaust than it had been before it, but so also was polonophobia. The prejudices and tensions between both sides persisted as a feature of Polish political life and social attitudes, though with perhaps diminishing intensity, until the end of the Communist era in 1989/90, and beyond.[46]

NOTES

1. Helen Fein, *Accounting for Genocide: National Responses and Jewish Victimization during the Holocaust* (Free Press, New York, 1979), pp. 33, 50 ff.

2. Antony Polonsky (ed.), *'My Brother's Keeper?'* *Recent Polish Debates on the Holocaust* (Routledge, London, 1990), Introduction.
3. Polish–Jewish Relations During the Second World War. A Discussion', *Polin*, 2 (1987), comment by Yisrael Gutman, p. 341.
4. Andrzej Chojnowski, 'The Jewish Community of the Second Republic in Polish Historiography of the 1980s', *Polin*, 1 (1986), pp. 288–99; Antony Polonsky, 'Polish–Jewish Relations and the Holocaust', *Polin*, 4 (1989), pp. 226–42, especially pp. 228–31.
5. Yisrael Gutman, 'Polish and Jewish Historiography on the Question of Polish–Jewish Relations during World War II', in Chimen Abramsky, Maciej Jachimczyk and Antony Polonsky (eds), *The Jews in Poland* (Basil Blackwell, Oxford, 1986), pp. 177–89; Shmuel Krakowski, 'Relations Between Jews and Poles during the Holocaust: New and Old Approaches in Polish Historiography', *Yad Vashem Studies*, 19 (1988), pp. 317–40; Ezra Mendelsohn, *Zionism in Poland: The Formative Years, 1915–1926* (Yale University Press, New Haven, 1981); Emmanuel Ringelbaum, *Polish–Jewish Relations during the Second World War* (Northwestern University Press, Evanston, 1992).
6. *The Times*, 21 February 1998, reports that a large cross commemorating a landmark Mass celebrated by the Pope in 1979 is to be removed from its location near Auschwitz because of protests from Jewish groups. Smaller crosses were removed in December 1997 from the Auschwitz museum following similar protests.
7. Jan Błonski, *Tygodnik Powszechny*, 11 January 1987, reprinted in English as 'The Poor Poles Look at the Ghetto', *Polin*, 2 (1987), pp. 321–36; see also comments on the article by Polonsky, 'Polish–Jewish Relations', *Polin*, 4 (1989), esp. pp. 231–3, and Norman Davies, 'Ethnic Diversity in Twentieth-Century Poland', *ibid.*, p. 155.
8. See Chapter 3 in this book.
9. Adolf Hitler, *Mein Kampf* (Hutchinson, London, 1969), especially pp. 258–99, 402–10.
10. See Martin Broszat, *The Hitler State* (Longman, London, 1981), Ian Kershaw, *The Nazi Dictatorship* (Edward Arnold, London, 1993); *idem, Hitler* (Longman, London, 1991); Eberhard Jäckel, *Hitler's Weltanschauung: A Blueprint for Power* (Wesleyan University Press, Middletown, Conn., 1972); Alan Bullock, *Hitler and Stalin: Parallel Lives* (Harper Collins, London, 1991); Gerald Fleming, *Hitler and the Final Solution* (University of California Press, Berkeley, 1984); Sarah Gordon, *Hitler, Germans and the 'Jewish Question'* (Princeton University Press, Princeton, NJ, 1984).
11. Hermann Graml, *Anti-semitism in the Third Reich* (Blackwell, Oxford, 1992), provides a well-informed and succinct overview.
12. Detailed accounts in the Polish Ministry of Information, *The German New Order in Poland* (Hutchinson, London, 1942) and Jan T. Gross, *Polish Society under German Occupation: The Generalgouvernement, 1939–1944* (Princeton University Press, Princeton, NJ, 1979). A useful reference work is Walter Okoński, *Wartime Poland,*

1939–1945: A Select Bibliography (Greenwood Press, New York, 1997).

13. From a vast literature, see Peter Hoffmann, *Widerstand, Staatsstreich, Attentat. Der Kampf der Opposition gegen Hitler* (Piper, Munich, 1969), *idem, German Resistance to Hitler* (Harvard University Press, Cambridge, Mass., 1988).

14. Stefan Korboński, *The Jews and the Poles in World War II* (Hippocrene Press, New York, 1989), pp. 45, 68; further details in Władysław Bartoszewski and Zofia Lewinówna, *The Samaritans: Heroes of the Holocaust* (New York, 1970); *idem* (eds), *Righteous Among Nations: How Poles Helped the Jews, 1939–1945* (Earls Court Publications, London, 1969); Kazimierz Iranek-Osmecki, *He Who Saves One Life* (Crown Publishers, New York, 1971); Nechama Tec, *Christian Rescue of Jews in Nazi-Occupied Poland* (Oxford University Press, London, 1985). A figure of only 60,000 Jews saved by Poles is given in Teresa Prekerowa, ' "Sprawiedliwi" i "bierni" ', *Tygodnik Powszechny*, 29 March 1987.

15. Stefan Korboński, *The Polish Underground State: A Guide to the Underground, 1939–1945* (Columbia University Press, New York, 1978); Teresa Prekerowa, 'The Relief Council for Jews in Poland, 1942–1945', in Abramsky *et al.* (eds), *Jews in Poland*, pp. 161–76.

16. Yisrael Gutman, *The Jews of Warsaw, 1939–1943: Ghetto, Underground, Revolt* (Indiana University Press, Bloomington, 1982); Shmuel Krakowski, *The War of the Doomed: Jewish Armed Resistance in Poland, 1942–1944* (Holmes & Meier, New York, 1984).

17. Lucjan Dobroszycki, *Reptile Journalism: The Official Polish-language Press Under the Nazis, 1939–1945* (Yale University Press, New Haven, 1994), *passim*.

18. Krakowski, 'Relations Between Jews and Poles during the Holocaust', p. 327.

19. Ringelblum, *Polish–Jewish Relations*, p. 247.

20. Yisrael Gutman and Shmuel Krakowski, *Unequal Victims: Poles and Jews During World War II* (New York, 1986), pp. 120–34, 216–20.

21. J. L. Armstrong, 'The Polish Underground and the Jews: A Reassessment of Home Army Commander Tadeusz Bór-Komorowski's Order 116 Against Banditry', *Slavonic and East European Review*, 72 (1994), No. 2, pp. 259–76.

22. Jaff Schatz, *The Generation: The Rise and Fall of the Jewish Communists of Poland* (University of California Press, Berkeley, 1991), pp. 152 ff.; Ben-Cion Pinchuk, *Shtetl Jews under Soviet Rule: Eastern Poland on the Eve of the Holocaust* (Blackwell, Oxford, 1990). The 1931 national census recorded a Jewish population in Eastern Poland of 925,000 from a total of 11 million, according to Adam Żółtowski, *Border of Europe: A Study of the Polish Eastern Provinces* (Hollis & Carter, London, 1950), pp. 286–91.

23. Ryszard Terlecki, 'The Jewish Issue in the Polish Army in the USSR and the Near East, 1941–1944', in Norman Davies and

Antony Polonsky (eds), *Jews in Eastern Poland and the USSR, 1939–46* (Macmillan, London, 1991), pp. 161–71; Władysław Anders, *Bez Ostatniego Rozdziału* (Gryf, London, 1983), p. 99.

24. Keith Sword, *Deportation and Exile: Poles in the Soviet Union, 1939–48* (Macmillan, London, 1994), pp. 1–27.

25. Davies and Polonsky (eds), *Jews in Eastern Poland*, pp. 6, 12 ff.; full details in Keith Sword (ed.), *The Soviet Takeover of the Polish Eastern Provinces, 1939–41* (Macmillan, London, 1991); Jan T. Gross, *Revolution from Abroad: The Soviet Conquest of Poland's Western Ukraine and Western Byelorussia* (Princeton University Press, Princeton, NJ, 1988). A specious apologetic for Jewish behaviour is given in Paweł Korzec and Jean-Charles Szurek, 'Jews and Poles under Soviet Occupation (1939–1941)', *Polin*, 4 (1989), pp. 204–25.

26. M. K. Dziewanowski, *The Communist Party of Poland* (Harvard University Press, Cambridge, Mass., 1976), pp. 98–100, 126, 154; Jan B. de Weydenthal, *The Communists of Poland* (Hoover Institution Press, Stanford, 1978), pp. 17–19, 26 f.

27. The argument adduced by Jan T. Gross, 'The Sovietization of Western Ukraine and Western Byelorussia', in Davis and Polonsky (eds), *Jews in Eastern Poland*, pp. 60–76.

28. Jan Karski, *The Story of a Secret State* (Boston, 1944), pp. 77–106.

29. Roman Zimand, 'Wormwood and Ashes (Do Poles and Jews Hate Each Other?)', *Polin*, 4 (1989), p. 339.

30. Examples provided in Manfred Kridl, Jerzy Wittlin and Władysław Malinowski, *The Democratic Hertiage of Poland* (Allen & Unwin, London, 1944), p. 224.

31. *Ibid.*, pp. 197–8.

32. David Engel, *In the Shadow of Auschwitz: The Polish Government-in-Exile and the Jews, 1939–1942* (University of North Carolina Press, Chapel Hill, 1987), pp. 80 ff.

33. Korboński, *Jews and Poles*, p. 83.

34. Engel, *Shadow*, pp. 83–113.

35. David Engel, *Facing a Holocaust: The Polish Government-in-Exile and the Jews, 1943–1945* (University of North Carolina Press, Chapel Hill, 1993), pp. 70 ff. 84, 203 ff.

36. Gutman, 'Polish and Jewish Historiography ...', in Abramsky *et al.* (eds), *Jews in Poland*, pp. 184–5.

37. Engel, *Facing a Holocaust*, pp. 162–5, 177 ff., 281.

38. Korboński, *Jews and Poles*, p. 55.

39. Richard C. Lukas, *The Forgotten Holocaust: The Poles under German Occupation, 1939–1944* (University Press of Kentucky, Lexington, 1986).

40. Ringelbaum, *Polish–Jewish Relations*, p. 315.

41. Polish Government-in-Exile, *The Yalta Agreements*, ed. Zygmunt C. Szkopiak (London, 1986), provides good coverage of important documents; Sikorski Historical Institute, *Documents on Polish–Soviet Relations, 1939–1945* (Heinemann, London, 1961).

42. Antony Polonsky and Bolesław Drukier, *The Beginnings of Communist Rule in Poland, December 1943–June 1945* (Routledge, London, 1980), pp. 90–128; see also Krystyna Kersten, *The Establishment of Communist Rule in Poland, 1943–1948* (London, 1993); Teresa Torańska, *'Them': Stalin's Polish Puppets* (New York, 1987). The wider picture is discussed in N. M. Naimark and L. Gibianskii, *The Establishment of Communist Regimes in Eastern Europe, 1944–1949* (Westview Press, Boulder, Co., 1996). On the issue of elections, see William Larch, 'Yalta and the American Approach to Free Elections in Poland', *The Polish Review*, 40 (1995), No. 3, pp. 267–80.

43. Michal Borwicz, 'Polish–Jewish Relations, 1944–1947', in Abramsky *et al.* (eds), *Jews in Poland*, pp. 190–1.

44. Korboński, *Jews and Poles*, pp. 73 ff., 79 ff., 84 ff.; Norman Davies, *Heart of Europe: A Short History of Poland* (Clarendon Press, Oxford, 1984), p. 149.

45. In Michael C. Steinlauf, *Bondage to the Dead: Poland and the Memory of the Holocaust* (Syracuse University Press, Syracuse, 1996), the Poles are criticised for failing even to make an effort to come to terms with the meaning of the Holocaust.

46. Lukasz Hirszowicz, 'The Jewish Issue in Post-War Communist Politics', in Abramsky *et al.* (eds), *Jews in Poland*, pp. 199–208.

7 The Polish Minority in Scotland: 1945 until the Present

The end of the Second World War brought mixed emotions and experiences for members of the Polish Armed Forces in the West who had fought under British military command to free their country from Nazi occupation and repression. While enjoying with their long-standing Allies the euphoria of military victory over the Third Reich, the Poles quickly discovered that it was accompanied by a stunning political defeat which determined their long-term fate.

From 1945 until the early 1950s the Polish population of Scotland and the UK as a whole fluctuated in size and composition as a consequence of demobilization, repatriation, emigration and resettlement, involving not only military personnel and their dependants, but also refugees, displaced persons, former prisoners of war and concentration-camp inmates from across Europe, former conscripted labour from Germany (*Organisation Todt*) and the category known as European Voluntary Workers. At its highest point during the early post-war years the total number of Poles in the UK was approximately 250,000, with a substantial though rapidly diminishing minority in Scotland. According to the National Census of 1951 there were at that time 10,603 Polish-born persons in Scotland. Males outnumbered females by a ratio of about 6 to 1, and the overwhelming majority of both were under 40 years of age. The UK figure for the Polish-born population was 162,339.[1] Clearly, therefore, a basis had been laid for the development of a significant Polish community in Scotland and elsewhere in the UK.

The factors which decisively influenced that development were multifarious. Regretfully, many were also inauspicious. In particular, two fundamental attitudes were very much in evidence during these early post-war years. First, the vast majority of Poles did not want to be in Scotland or anywhere else in the UK, and regarded their sojourn, therefore, as merely temporary. They wanted to be in the free and independent Poland for which they had fought from the beginning to the end of the war. Second, neither the British government, particularly the Foreign Secretary, Ernest Bevin, nor the British public at large wanted the Poles to remain in the UK. At the end of the war, the universal expectation was that the Polish troops would be repatriated *en masse*.[2]

These negative attitudes on both sides were exacerbated by a series of developments, some of which had been in the making during the course of the war.

In the first instance, the Poles in the UK felt betrayed by the political outcome of the war. Feelings of acute bitterness, anger, resentment, contempt and disillusionment were directed at their ertswhile British and American allies. Their considerable military contribution to the Allied war effort, beginning with the role of Polish airmen in the Battle of Britain, and subsequently encompassing, for example, the exploits in Normandy and the Low Countries of the First Polish Armoured Division under General Stanisław Maczek, and of the Second Polish Corps in Italy under General Władysław Anders, had apparently counted for nothing in the end.[3] The cause of a Free Poland, as represented by the Polish Government in London, led until his death in July 1943 by General Władysław Sikorski,[4] had been systematically compromised and then finally abandoned by the British Prime Minister, Winston Churchill, and the American President, Franklin D. Roosevelt.[5]

From the moment the Soviet Union joined Britain and the USA in the Grand Alliance, in 1941, the Western leaders had been prepared to sacrifice Polish interests in order to keep Stalin on side. The Soviets were considered to be crucial to victory over Hitler, while the Poles were not, and the fact that Stalin had been an ally of Nazi Germany for two years previously was forgotten as a matter of political and military expediency.

Consequently, the Polish national interest, as understood by Sikorski's government and its many supporters in Poland, was progressively marginalized until it was ultimately ignored altogether. Upon its discovery in April 1943, the Katyń Massacre had been played down by Churchill, and this type of behaviour that was inimical to the Polish cause continued most obviously at the Tehran Conference in December the same year, with particular reference to Poland's eastern territories, which the Soviets had coveted since their defeat by the Poles in 1920.[6] Finally and conclusively, the Poles fell victim to the agenda at both the Yalta and Potsdam Conferences in 1945. The failure, moreover, of the Warsaw Uprising by the Home Army (AK), in August 1944, had been a comprehensive political, military and diplomatic catastrophe for the London Poles from which they had never recovered.[7] In 1944–5, therefore, there was no effective opposition from within or outside Poland to Stalin's designs for it.

Accordingly, and with Western connivance, the Soviet Union was allowed to annex 40 per cent of the territory of the pre-war Polish Republic, including the historic Polish cities of Lwów and Wilno, and at the same time to establish its military and political hegemony over the remainder of a country where, historically, Communism had enjoyed only the most insignificant popular support.[8] This betrayal was consummated on 5 July 1945 when the British and American governments withdrew their official recognition from the Polish Government in London, while simultaneously recognizing the Communist-dominated, Soviet-imposed Provisional Government of National Unity (TRJN) in Warsaw. This was to add appalling insult to grievous injury, of course, and no less objectionable from a Polish viewpoint was the decision of the British government, acting under pressure from Stalin and the Warsaw Communists, to ban Polish military units from participating in the VE parade in London.

It soon also became clear that the British Labour government under Clement Attlee, which had assumed office in July 1945, was making every possible effort to cooperate with the Warsaw regime and Stalin, while pointedly distancing itself from the remnants of the derecognized Free Polish Government in London. Thus, in August 1945, the government insisted on the dismissal of General Tadeusz Bór-Komorowski, Commander-in-Chief of the Polish Armed Forces in the West and former Commander of the Home Army (AK), because his anti-Communist and anti-Soviet views were considered a serious impediment to Britain's efforts to improve relations with Stalin.[9] Moreover, in March 1946, partly at least under pressure from the Communist-dominated regime in Warsaw, the British decided, without consulting the

Poles, to disband the Polish military units in the UK, withdraw financial support from the derecognized government and reduce its administrative structure to the bare bones. Polish soldiers were encouraged to return home, and contact between the London Poles and their supporters in Poland was discouraged by the British through every available means. At the same time there was virtual silence about the reign of terror being unleashed in Poland by the Soviet Secret Police (NKVD) and their Polish Communist allies against 'oppositional elements', while in January 1947 the British made only muted protests about the gross irregularities and abuses which accompanied the elections in Poland.[10]

All these events and developments were the 'reward' for the Poles of six years of the most abject suffering, exhausting combat and faithful adherence to the Allied cause. Could anyone really blame them for their jaundiced outlook and antagonism towards the British? For them, unfortunately, the concept of 'Perfidious Albion' had become an all-too-painful reality.[11] In Scotland, it was noted that their 'bitterness arising from the failure of all their hopes, steadily worsening news from Poland, and lack of family life' was driving many Poles to utter despair, and even to 'abandonment of religious observance'.[12]

Until the onset of the Cold War at the end of the 1940s and early 1950s, Britain witnessed a prodigious wave of admiration and enthusiasm for the Soviet Union, the valiant ally against Nazi tyranny, and in particular for 'Uncle Joe' Stalin, who had masterminded his country's war effort alongside the Western Powers. This sentiment was by no means confined to left-wing circles of the Labour Party and the Trade Unions, but also enveloped sections of the Establishment, including the BBC, the conservative press and Foreign Office. Among the most vehemently pro-Soviet and anti-Polish elements were the later well-known left-wing historians, E. H. Carr, political editor of *The Times* during the war and special adviser to Churchill, and Christopher Hill, an influential official in the Foreign Office. Pro-Soviet propaganda from these circles had been gathering momentum since the formation of the Grand Alliance, and four years later had reached fever pitch.[13] By then the initial goodwill displayed towards the Poles after their arrival in Scotland in 1940, when they had been welcomed and fêted as the gallant underdogs now standing alongside Britain against Hitler's Germany, had been almost entirely dissipated, to be replaced by a palpable hostility which endured for some years in official government and high political circles, and among many ordinary people for much longer still.[14]

In broader perspective, this signified a reversion, albeit in intensified form, to the unfriendly attitudes, epitomized by Prime Minister David Lloyd George at the Paris Peace Conference in 1919 and later, which Britain had adopted towards Poland during the inter-war years. The British Guarantee of March 1939, the Anglo–Polish Alliance and Britain's declaration of war when Poland was invaded in September 1939, were all radical departures from the norm of Anglo–Polish relations.[15]

Primarily because of their ill-concealed anti-Soviet and anti-Communist views, the Poles were regularly denigrated, especially in Scotland, as 'fascists', 'warmongers', 'landlords', and 'anti-Semites' – all left-wing-inspired opprobrious epithets that were eagerly taken up by wider sections of society.[16] The Poles were expected by a substantial section of public opinion, and frequently exhorted by the British government,[17] to return home to help rebuild their own country, despite deteriorating political conditions in Poland, and to cease being a burden, therefore, on the British Treasury. Rumours of Polish blackmarketeering and petty criminality, which were invariably exaggerated, further poisoned the atmosphere. Sections of the popular press, notably the Express Group, owned by the polonophobic Lord Beaverbrook, and *The Daily Worker*, stridently encouraged this animosity towards the Poles. For good measure, *The Times* also often felt obliged, in line with the overall thrust of government policy, to praise the Warsaw regime. In Scotland, however, *The Scotsman* proved to be an honourable exception by evincing a generally sympathetic understanding of the Free Poles and their predicament.[18]

The Poles themselves lacked the means, organization and support to counter effectively this unseemly propaganda, which in central Scotland could also assume blatant sectarian overtones. The fact that a substantial majority of the Poles were Catholic made them a conspicuous and vulnerable target for sections of a society where the Church of Scotland, exuding a still rather strict

Presbyterianism, with its inherent anti-Irish and anti-Catholic animus, as well as the overtly sectarian Orange Order, continued to exercise a considerable influence. This may be illustrated, for example, by the Kirk's official sponsorship from the mid-1920s until at least the late 1930s of a campaign against the presence of Irish Catholics in Scotland which employed language and propaganda of unequivocal racist-fascist connotations. Powerful echoes of this attitude survived the war, especially at a popular, grass-roots level in sections of the Protestant community.[19] Indeed, it was an extremist group, the so-called Protestant Action Society led by John Cormack, that organized the first anti-Polish rally in Edinburgh's Usher Hall in June 1946.[20] Local branches of the National Union of Mineworkers (NUM) in Scotland, especially in the west-central belt and Ayrshire, had strong links with local Orange lodges, and emerged, therefore, as notable centres of bitterness towards the Catholic Poles.[21] The Polish Press Agency, based in Edinburgh and headed by Zygmunt Nagórski, sought to counter this barrage of hatred; but, small and poorly resourced, it made little headway.[22]

Even if their stay in Scotland was deemed temporary, the Poles still had to make important adjustments to a society which was in many respects very different from that of pre-war Poland. Poland had been overwhelmingly rural and agrarian; its social conventions and customs, culture, religion, and politics bore little or no resemblance to these elements in Scotland and the UK; and for the Poles there was the added difficulty of coping with a completely different language.[23] French had been the primary foreign language for educated Poles before the war, reflecting the historically close ties between the two countries, so that in 1945 relatively few Poles spoke English of a reasonable standard. And, naturally, the Scottish dialect constituted a formidable challenge on its own account.

In addition, the Poles were having to make these adjustments in a Britain that was itself trying to find its feet following a war that had bankrupted her and accelerated an inexorable process of loss of status and influence in the wider world. The American 'Lend-Lease' scheme ended suddenly in August 1945, and post-war austerity, including a shortage of housing and rationing, only served to increase tensions between the indigeneous population and the Polish newcomers. The root problem, of course, was long-entrenched British xenophobia, a dislike and suspicion of 'bloody foreigners'. Although the incidence of outright violence between the two sides in Scotland was low, there were persistent undercurrents that regularly found expression in rude behaviour, name-calling and gratuitous insults towards the Poles, including the sneering exhortation, 'Go back to Poland'.

The Poles suffered from their lack of official status in Britain. Apart from the 8,691 who had been naturalized by 1950, they were stateless. They were not citizens of the UK, and some, especially former high-ranking army officers, had been stripped of their Polish citizenship by the Warsaw regime out of political spite. General Maczek was the most prominent casualty in this respect in Scotland. As alien immigrants, the Poles were issued with an Aliens' Registration Certificate.[24] In practice, this meant that they were obliged to report regularly to their local police station to confirm their place of abode and employment – a practice which continued well into the 1950s. Any lapses would entail a visit by the police to the home of the offender or a summons to the local police station. There is evidence to suggest that these encounters were not always conducted in an entirely constructive manner by the police, particularly in areas of sectarian tension like Glasgow and its environs.[25]

The inability to settle down in their new surroundings was compounded by the belief of many Poles that further conflict between the West and the Soviet Union was inevitable, and would see them recalled to the colours to complete the struggle for a Free Poland. Political and military leaders such as General Anders, possibly the most defiantly anti-Communist personality in the Polish ranks in the UK, encouraged the view that Polish military personnel had been not so much demobbed as put on 'indefinite leave', awaiting the call in the near future.[26] This attitude by itself nurtured among most Poles a feeling of transience, of 'killing time'. Psychologically, it created formidable barriers, at the very least, to their acceptance of Scotland or the UK as their permanent home.

Finally, the Poles themselves could be said to have contributed to some extent to their problems by continuing to indulge, as before and during the war, in a good deal of internecine squabbling. Political, ethnic and social relations in inter-war Poland had been somewhat fractured, and Sikorski's wartime government had been riven by factionalism, which only worsened after 1943 under his less able and commanding successors, Stanisław Mikołajczyk (1943–4) and Tomasz Arciszewski (1944–7).[27] After 1945, Poles divided on whether to return to a Communist-dominated Poland, where many had family, on how far to trust the Warsaw regime, and to what extent they should continue to respect the now unofficial Polish government in London. At least they were all united, except for an exiguous pro-Communist minority, in rejecting Yalta. But otherwise, political and personal differences produced bad feeling in the embryonic Polish community, particularly following the death in June 1947 of Władysław Raczkiewicz, who had been President of the Polish Government-in-Exile since 1939. As an exasperated observer noted:

> The Poles have always brought a great deal of their troubles on their heads through their internal dissensions – this has been the case for centuries back. I have found the Piłsudskiites and Sikorskiites as hostile to each other as both are to the Russians.[28]

It would be misleading, however, to depict the Poles' situation as one of unmitigated gloom. For one thing, there were always acts of individual kindness towards them by Scots which were deeply appreciated. Polish soldiers who were billeted with Scots families during the war often formed lasting friendships which transcended post-war difficulties.

More substantively, in Scotland, and despite the constant movement of Poles to other locations both in the UK and abroad, the early post-war years already saw the emergence of Polish communities in major centres, such as Edinburgh, Glasgow, Falkirk, Dundee and Kirkcaldy, though Poles could also be found widely scattered throughout the country. Employment opportunities, the location of resettlement camps and wartime attachments all helped determine the pattern of residence. For example, the National Census of 1951 recorded approximately 1,200 Polish-born persons living in Edinburgh, 1,100 in Glasgow, 300 in Dundee and 210 in Falkirk.[29]

Scotland's capital attracted a high proportion of former army officers and professional types, many of whom had served in General Maczek's First Armoured Division and followed the General in settling in Edinburgh. Consequently, the Polish community that took shape there had a strong middle-class character that immediately marked it out from other Polish communities, where persons from a poorly educated peasant or working-class background formed a clear majority. All parts of pre-war Poland were represented in the émigré community, though a large percentage originated from the eastern territories that had been incorporated into the Soviet Union in 1945, meaning that they had no homes to return to. Most of them, however, shared, to one degree or another, a devotion to traditional patriotic, anti-Communist and Catholic values, and an equally powerful determination to defend these against assimilationist tendencies. Polish organizations of various kinds were quickly set up, including branches of the Polish Ex-Combatants' Association (SPK). A Polish press, which had appeared as soon as Polish troops had arrived in Scotland in 1940, continued to operate at various levels, and Polish priests were soon on hand, with Father Ludwik Bombas emerging as the Rector of the Polish Catholic Mission in Scotland.[30]

Moreover, because of a serious labour shortage, which had been underlined by the severe winter of 1946–7, the Poles found it easier by the following year to find employment, even if it often meant taking on the heaviest and dirtiest unskilled manual jobs. Before then, trade union opposition to the employment of Poles had been vociferously expressed by the NUM, the National Union of Farmworkers and the Amalgamated Union of Engineering Workers (AUEW), not only on grounds of competition in the labour market, but also for political, ideological and, in Scotland, sectarian reasons.[31] In time, the unions, with the notable exception of the AUEW, came to grudgingly accept the Poles as a 'necessary evil'. More importantly, the British government, realizing with considerable regret that large numbers of Poles were likely to remain in the UK for some time, introduced the Polish Resettlement Corps (PRC) in September 1946, when some 36,000 Polish troops were still stationed in Scotland. Complemented by the Polish Resettlement Act of March 1947, this scheme was designed to facilitate the introduction of Polish ex-servicemen into useful civilian life and employment. Despite considerable difficulties, particularly with hard-line Polish 'recalcitrants', by the time it was wound up in September 1949 the PRC had largely fufilled this aim, though it involved the transfer of most Poles from Scotland to England and Wales.[32]

For certain categories of Poles, however, the transition to civvy street was especially traumatic. For most of the former officer and professional classes it proved virtually impossible to obtain employment commensurate with their previous qualifications and social status, so that they ended up as 'displaced professionals' in manual labour or in petty self-employment in a new field, such as watch-repairing, shoemaking and photography. Many former lawyers, teachers, civil servants and civil engineers, for example, had this painful and humiliating experience.[33] The most notorious case was that of General Maczek who, following demobilization in 1948 at the age of 56, was obliged to take up a series of low-grade jobs, including that of bartending in a hotel owned by one of his former soldiers. This disgraceful treatment of a legendary personality, one of the most successful and highly decorated Allied commanders of the war, was widely interpreted in the Polish community as yet one more manifestation of the British government's scant regard for its former loyal ally.[34]

On the other hand, it has to be said that the Poles would have been much worse off had they returned to a Soviet-controlled, Communist Poland, where secret police terror, deportations to the Gulag, wholesale murder, political trials, and a cavalier disregard for human rights were the order of the day.[35] This was the new 'Socialist paradise' into which a disturbingly large proportion of the 105,000 Poles who did return from Scotland and the UK disappeared, never to be heard of again.[36] In Scotland, despite many problems and hardships, the Poles enjoyed a higher standard of living than they would have had in Poland, especially in view of the newly introduced welfare state; and they were living in an open, if not entirely friendly, democratic society.

Among the few organized friends the Poles did have were the hierarchy and press of the Catholic Church, which had generally supported the cause of a Free Poland since 1940.[37] On 4 August 1944, for example, the Catholic hierarchy of Scotland issued a Manifesto, warning of the Communist and Soviet threat to Poland in direct opposition to government policy.[38] Poles were welcomed in Catholic parishes, though it was by no means always the case that the rank and file of the laity, of predominantly Irish origin, exhibited the same degree of warmth towards them as the bishops or prominent figures such as Sir Patrick J. Dollan, Lord Provost of Glasgow. Increased intermarriage between Polish men and Scottish women, which had by August 1945 produced about 2,000 unions, helped break down barriers over time.[39] None the less, anti-Polish sentiment in Scottish society as a whole persisted for much longer, especially in extreme Protestant circles, despite the efforts of organizations such as the Scottish–Polish Society to foster a healthier climate of mutual respect.

Established in 1941 with branches throughout Scotland, attracting in its heyday during the war several thousand members from a broad range of the Scottish social spectrum as well as from Polish exiles,[40] the Society boasted in its ranks several prominent public figures and some aristocrats, such as Lady Campbell Black, Lord Inverclyde, the Earl of Elgin and, from the University of Glasgow, Sir Hector Hetherington.[41] Often with the assistance of these connections, the Society lobbied vigorously, if not always successfully, in the Polish interest, for example over Poland's right to be reconstituted at the end of the war with her 1939 border in the East protected from Soviet encroachment.[42] By the late 1940s the Society had developed under the powerful leadership of Glasgow solicitor, John J. Campbell, as a staunch defender of the Free Poles against attacks from left-wing, extreme Protestant and Jewish circles, as well as from a large volume of virulent propaganda from the Warsaw regime.[43] A noted *bête noire* was the Communist Polish Consul General in Scotland, based in Glasgow, a Mr Teliga, who was denounced, with good reason, as a veritable *agent provocateur*.[44] None the less, the Society's efficacy inevitably diminished as its members drifted away and the tide of public opinion turned against the Poles.

By the early 1950s most Poles had come to accept that there would be no further military campaign to liberate Poland from the grip of Soviet-imposed Communism and that, unfortunately, their exile in Scotland was permanent. Their overall situation in a foreign country was far from settled or comfortable, but they had to meet the new challenge of carving out a useful niche for themselves and their families. In the space of a tumultuous decade they had been uprooted by war, occupation and genocide from their beloved Poland,[45] fought gallantly on many fronts for their freedom and that of others, in the traditional Polish fashion, but had then found that they had been ruthlessly stabbed in the back by so-called Allies when it mattered. If many Poles in Scotland had, therefore, a justifiably unfavourable view of their hosts, and were made acutely to feel like 'outsiders', they had little option but to get on with their lives as best they could.

Between 1951 and 1981 it was officially recorded that the number of persons resident in Scotland who had been born in Poland had declined from 10,603 to 5,083. During the 1950s a large number of Poles had either migrated to England or emigrated overseas in search of better job opportunities, while others had simply died. Only a minority had returned to Poland. In the decade following the 1981 Census, the natural cycle resulted in this first Polish generation being reduced to 3,623, a figure lowered much further during the 1990s.[46] At the same time the wider Polish community had been replenished by family growth, producing a second and third generation of Polish background, and by a limited number of Poles who managed or were permitted to leave Poland during the Communist era, including some who came as political refugees, for example, following the imposition of martial law in Poland in December 1981. By the mid-1990s the entire Polish community was reckoned to number approximately 10,000.[47]

In the post-war period the gender imbalance in the Polish community, as indicated, for example, in the 1951 census, when of 1,200 Polish-born persons in Edinburgh, 895 were male, and of 1,164 in Glasgow, 975, inevitably meant that intermarriage with Scottish women was widespread. This certainly helped the Poles to assimilate, especially if, as was not uncommon, the Polish male partner adopted the surname of his spouse, or decided to anglicize his Polish name. In these ethnically and, as was often also the case, confessionally mixed marriages, the invariable use of English at home promoted assimilation, so that most children of such unions did not learn to speak Polish, despite the establishment in these years of Saturday-morning instruction classes in Polish language which were run by Polish organizations. For instance, in Glasgow, where a Polish parish had been set up in 1948 under Father Jan Gruszka, a Polish School followed a few years later; and other schools appeared in Johnstone, Edinburgh, Falkirk and elsewhere.[48]

By that time a large number of Poles, accepting that their exile was permanent, withdrew from active participation in Polish community life. Their decision was also prompted by the divisions which surfaced among the largest concentration of Poles, in London, when in the mid-1950s the so-called *Zamek,* followers of the President of the Polish Government-in-Exile, August Zaleski, who had been Foreign Minister of the Second Republic from 1926 until 1932,[49] clashed with the *Zjednoczenie* (Federation) led by General Władysław Anders.[50] As a consequence of these disagreements a number of new Polish groups were formed, including the Polish Social and Educational Society (*Dom Sikorskiego*) in Glasgow[51] and the Polish War Disabled Union (*Dom Inwalidy*) in Edinburgh, in opposition to the Polish Ex-Combatants' Association (SPK) which had led support for the *Zjednoczenie.* Paradoxically, perhaps, the Poles who were then most discouraged by this development from taking further active part in Polish community life were often amongst the most patriotic, who felt the pain of exile and internecine squabbling so much that their coping strategy was simply to try to integrate into Scottish society as far as possible, while privately maintaining their devotion to a Poland for which they had fought so valiantly in vain. While outwardly many did assimilate, however, it was usually to a limited extent and they remained, beneath the surface, deeply committed to Poland and her traditional patriotic values. While their vision of pre-war Poland may have been coloured by nostalgia, and accentuated by an inclination to compare it flatteringly with many aspects of Scottish society, they also derived a strength from this outlook which facilitated their efforts to create a worthwhile life in exile.

As the Poles settled down into employment and family life, those in Central Scotland became fully acquainted with the less salubrious aspects of the Scottish scene, especially anti-Catholic sectarianism, which was particularly manifest in Glasgow and Lanarkshire, with their strong Orange and Masonic traditions. Moreover, the Catholic Poles did not endear themselves to their Scottish Protestant workmates because they generally wanted to work hard and make the most of their opportunities: being 'sent to Coventry' by them for nothing more than honest endeavour made a poignant commentary on the everyday observance of working-class Presbyterianism. Complaints to union officials about the Poles' work ethic were quite frequent, and steps were often taken to ensure that well-earned promotion was denied them. The Socialist trade unions and the political parties were indifferent, at best, to this blatant discrimination.[52]

The organized Polish community kept a low profile in Scottish life. Its sense of identity was most obviously celebrated on certain anniversaries, such as Polish National Day on 3 May, Independence Day on 11 November, General Sikorski's death on 4 July, Polish Soldiers' Day on 15 August, and the annual pilgrimage in late August to the grotto at Carfin in Lanarkshire. But these were organized out of general public view and awareness. The media had no interest in them. Moreover, the various organizations that had sprung up were firmly controlled by the first generation of Poles, even into the late 1990s, with little attempt being made to encourage the second and third generations to assume any real degree of responsibility – a measure, undoubtedly, of the still profound sense of insecurity felt by older Poles, as well as a reflection of their inherently authoritarian outlook.[53]

If the Polish community claimed any sort of cohesion it was in relation to its attitude to the Communist regime in Warsaw. Led by the example of General Maczek, an unswervingly staunch anti-Communist, the community sympathized with the periodic manifestations of revolt against the imposed government in Poland, for instance during the riots in Poznań in 1956, in Gdańsk in 1970 and, more dramatically, when *Solidarność* appeared on the scene in 1980–1. None the less, over time, from the 1950s onwards, a small number of renegades and opportunists appeared among the Poles in Scotland, and some of them profited materially by tacitly recognizing and cooperating in different ways with that illegal regime. This often took the form of their entering into commercial agreements with Warsaw through the agency of the Polish Consulate in Glasgow (later sited in Edinburgh), which was ignored, if at all possible, by the vast majority because it was staffed by card-carrying Communists.

In the early 1970s, the Warsaw regime played a significant role in the creation of the Scottish–Polish Cultural Association in Glasgow and Edinburgh with the aim, partially realized, of using it as a vehicle for disseminating a positive view of Communist Poland in Scotland. This organization, whose membership was insignificant but determined, found enthusiastic support from a number of staff in at least one Scottish university, which also made formal contact with a similar institution in Poland, and from the small, insidious pro-Communist element in the wider Polish community. In the 1990s the discord sown by the Scottish–Polish Cultural Association led to the closure of the Polish club in Dundee,[54] and helped engender dissension among the Poles in Edinburgh and Glasgow. In reaction, at least one new organization – The Polish Society – arose in order to cherish the traditional patriotic ethos, albeit within an academic framework.[55]

The rise of *Solidarność* in the wake of the elevation to the Papacy in October 1978 of Karol Wojtyła, Archbishop of Kraków, as John Paul II, captured the imagination of most Poles in Scotland, especially of the younger elements of the community.[56] These events rekindled pride in being Polish and revived hopes that somehow they heralded another challenge to the Communist regime in Warsaw. The triumphant visit of the Pope to Scotland in summer 1982[57] put the seal on this reinvigorated outlook which transcended the imposition of martial law by General Wojciech Jaruzelski in December 1981. From that moment onwards, it was sensed that at last Communism was no longer invincible, a perception fully vindicated in 1989 when the regime collapsed in ignominy. The Polish community at that time, composed predominantly of the younger generations, rejoiced in this dramatic turn of events, which was underlined in December 1990, when, in an emotional, dignified and triumphant ceremony in Warsaw's Royal Castle, the last President of the Polish Government-in-Exile in London, Ryszard Kaczorowski, handed over the state insignia of the Second Republic to the new and democratically elected President of Poland, Lech Wałęsa.[58] The exiled Polish government was then quickly wound up, and in a further highly symbolic gesture towards the 'new' Poland, in September 1993, the remains of General Władysław Sikorski, the country's eminent wartime leader, were removed from Newark Cemetery, Nottinghamshire, and finally laid to rest in honour in Wawel Castle, Kraków.

The day of liberation from the 'Red Tyranny', yearned for so ardently since 1945 and so often disappointed, had finally arrived, or so it seemed. The apparent 'revolution' in Poland, however, had quite a few unexpected twists and turns in store as the 1990s unfolded, not least the return to power by way of parliamentary elections in Autumn 1993 of the regrouped former Communists in the Democratic Left Alliance (SLD) and, to the further dismay of many Poles and their Scottish friends, Wałęsa's defeat by a former Communist apparatchik, Aleksander Kwaśniewski, in the presidential elections of 1995. Total victory over the Communist *nomenklatura* in Poland has clearly not yet been accomplished.[59]

In the fifty or so years since the end of the Second World War, the Polish community in Scotland has experienced many painful vicissitudes, and has undergone a considerable transformation in composition and outlook. It has retained, none the less, an intrinsic resilience and self-belief which sections of the second and third generations may be expected to cultivate in the future. Almost all of them are well-integrated into Scottish society, having progressed through the educational system, with a number now occupying positions of responsibility and prominence in the public sector, while others have made their mark in the private business sector. Although their degree of attachment to Polish patriotic values may vary, and political divisions among them are not unimportant, they invariably share a wholesome awareness of a distinguished heritage.

An impressive initiative has been the foundation in September 1996 of The Polish Society as an academic discussion forum for

Polish history, culture and contemporary affairs, which has attracted members from both Polish and Scottish backgrounds. The Society has already established links with several universities and other research bodies, and organized successful meetings and conferences.[60] On the other hand, there are unmistakable signs that the organizational life of the Polish community is diminishing, as revealed by the closure during the 1990s of Polish centres in Perth, Dundee, Edinburgh, Alloa and Galashiels, the reduction of the SPK to about 500 members,[61] and the demise, after only three years, of an English-language quarterly newspaper aimed at Poles in Scotland and further afield.[62] In the new context provided by Poland's re-establishment as a free and independent country, therefore, the future lines of development of the Polish community in Scotland, and indeed in the United Kingdom as a whole, are not entirely clear or altogether promising.[63]

NOTES

The original, shorter version of this paper was delivered to 'Scots and Slavs: an International Colloquium', at the University of Dundee, 28–30 June 1997.

1. General Registry Office, Edinburgh. *Census 1951. Scotland.* Volume III. *General Volume* (HMSO, Edinburgh), pp. 55–6. For a broad survey of the post-war refugee problem in Europe see A. C. Bramwell (ed.), *Refugees in the Age of Total War* (Unwin Hyman, London, 1988).

2. K. Sword, with N. Davies and J. Ciechanowski, *The Formation of the Polish Community in Great Britain, 1939–1950* (School of Slavonic and East European Studies, University of London, 1989), pp. 79, 305.

3. Essential details in A. Suchcitz, *Poland's Contribution to the Allied Victory in the Second World War* (The Polish Ex-Combatants Association, London, 1995); A. Zamoyski, *The Forgotten Few: The Polish Air Force in the Second World War* (John Murray, London, 1995); T. Modelski, *The Polish Contribution to the Ultimate Allied Victory in the Second World War* (Privately published, Woking, 1986); J. Garliński, *Poland in the Second World War* (Macmillan, London, 1985).

4. P. D. Stachura, 'Władysław Sikorski: Soldier, Politician, Statesman 1881–1943', *Scottish Slavonic Review*, 21 (1993, Autumn), pp. 71–94;

and K. Sword (ed.), *Sikorski: Soldier and Statesman* (Orbis, London, 1990), for a comprehensive assessment.

5. Anglo–Polish relations are well covered by A. Polonsky (ed.), *The Great Powers and the Polish Question, 1941–1945* (Orbis, London, 1976); G. V. Kacewicz, *Great Britain, the Soviet Union, and the Polish Government-in-Exile (1939–1945)* (Nijhoff, The Hague, 1979); S. Zochowski, *British Policy in Relation to Poland in the Second World War* (Vantage Press, New York, 1988); J. Karski, *The Great Powers and Poland, 1919–1945: From Versailles to Yalta* (University Press of America, Washington DC, 1985); and A. J. Prażmowska, *Britain and Poland, 1939–1943: The Betrayed Ally* (CUP, 1995). On the specific theme of Allied leadership, see Warren Kimball, *Forged in War: Churchill, Roosevelt and the Second World War* (Harper Collins, London, 1997).

6. Informed analysis in N. Davies, *White Eagle, Red Star: The Polish–Soviet War, 1919–20* (Macdonald, London, 1972); A. Zamoyski, *The Battle for the Marchlands* (Columbia University Press, New York, 1981). The Polish–Soviet border agreed at the Treaty of Riga in March 1921 was never stable because of the unwillingness of the Soviets to accept it as definitive, while the British had always taken the view that their so-called 'Curzon Line' represented a more realistic compromise: the Poles vehemently disagreed.

7. J. K. Zawodny, *Death in the Forest: The Story of the Katyń Forest Massacre* (Macmillan, London, 1971); Polish Cultural Foundation, *The Crime of Katyń: Facts and Documents* (Caldra House, London, 1965); S. Korboński, *The Polish Underground State: A Guide to the Underground, 1939–1945* (Columbia University Press, New York, 1978); J. K. Zawodny, *Nothing but Honour: The Story of the Warsaw Uprising* (Macmillan, London, 1978); J. M. Ciechanowski, *The Warsaw Rising of 1944* (CUP, 1974); Z. C. Szkopiak (ed.), *The Yalta Agreements* (Polish Government-in-Exile, London, 1986), esp. pp. 30–48, 51–147; A. M. Cienciala, 'Great Britain and Poland Before and After Yalta (1943–1945): A Reassessment', *The Polish Review*, 40 (1995), No. 3, pp. 281–313.

8. A. Polonsky and B. Drukier, *The Beginnings of Communist Rule in Poland, December 1943–June 1945* (Routledge, London, 1980). The pre-war Polish Communist Party (KPP), which was outlawed, was disbanded on Stalin's orders in 1938. See M. K. Dziewanowski, *The Communist Party of Poland: An Outline of its History* (Harvard University Press, Cambridge, Mass., 1976), and J. B. Weydenthal, *The Communists of Poland: An Historical Outline* (Hoover Institution Press, Stanford, 1978).

9. Sword *et al.*, *Formation*, p. 235. Bór-Komorowski resigned on 18 September 1945. This episode had a clear precedent, for in September 1944 Prime Minister Winston Churchill had successfully demanded the resignation of Bór-Komorowski's predecessor, General Kazimierz Sosnkowski, who was outspokenly anti-Soviet.

10. K. Kersten, *The Establishment of Communist Rule in Poland, 1943–1948* (Macmillan, London, 1993); W. Larsh, 'Yalta and the American Approach to Free Elections in Poland', *The Polish Review*, 40 (1995), 3, pp. 267–80.

11. W. Anders, *An Army in Exile* (Nashville, 1981, reprint); T. Bór-Komorowski, *The Secret Army* (Nashville, 1984, reprint), which are both replete with bitter recriminations against the British.

12. The Thornton Private Papers (kindly donated to the Chairman of The Polish Society in 1997 by Mrs Irene Thornton, a distinguished activist over many years in Scottish–Polish affairs), correspondence file, letter of 27 April 1948 from the London-based Catholic Council for Polish Welfare to Mr John J. Campbell, Chairman of the Scottish-Polish Society.

13. Sword *et al.*, *Formation*, pp. 132, 143.

14. W. Tomaszewski, *Na Szkockiej Ziemi* (Caldra House, London, 1976), pp. 69–210, provides an informed survey of life for the Poles in wartime Scotland.

15. A. Polonsky, *Politics in Independent Poland, 1921–1939: The Crisis of Constitutional Government*, (OUP, 1976), pp. 136 ff.; R. F. Leslie (ed.), *The History of Poland since 1863* (CUP, 1983), pp. 133 ff.; N. Davies, 'Lloyd George and Poland, 1919–20', *Journal of Contemporary History*, 6 (1971), No. 1, pp. 132–54; S. Newman, *The British Guarantee to Poland, March 1939* (OUP, 1976).

16. T. Ziarski-Kernberg, 'The Polish Community in Scotland since 1945', in P. D. Stachura (ed.), *Themes of Modern Polish History* (The Polish Social and Educational Society, Glasgow, 1992), p. 72.

17. Sword *et al.*, *Formation*, pp. 201, 229 ff.

18. *Ibid.*, pp. 344–8; and selected reports – for example, on 24 October 1946 – and editorials in '*The Scotsman*', 1944–8.

19. The most recent vivid exposition of the anti-Catholic outlook of the Kirk at that time, and later, was provided in Scottish Television's 'Secret History' programme broadcast on 18 June 1997.

20. T. Kernberg, *The Polish Community in Scotland* (Ph.D., University of Glasgow, 1990), pp. 231 ff.

21. The Thornton Private Papers, correspondence for 1945–7 from Mr John J. Campbell of the Scottish–Polish Society to several fellow members.

22. *Ibid.*, letter of 29 January 1948 from Nagórski to Mr John J Campbell of the Scottish–Polish Society. Soon afterwards, Nagórski left for the United States. See his memoirs, *Wojna w Londynie* (Paris, 1966).

23. The flavour of these problems is conveyed in N. Davies, *God's Playground: A History of Poland. Volume II: 1795 to the Present* (Clarendon Press, Oxford, 1981), pp. 393–434; and in T. Wiles (ed.), *Poland Between the Wars, 1918–1939* (Indiana University Press, Bloomington), 1989.

24. Sword *et al.*, *Formation*, pp. 314 f., 472.

25. Based on the personal recollections of a number of members of the Polish community in the Glasgow area intimated to the author.

26. Anders, *Army in Exile*, p. 350.
27. In Scotland, two internment camps for anti-Sikorski Polish army offi-
     cers were set up, in Rothesay, Isle of Bute, and Tighnabruaich.
28. The Thornton Private Papers, correspondence file of the Scottish–Polish
     Society, letter of 19 February 1948 from Mr J. Stewart of Edinburgh
     to Mr John J. Campbell. The 'Piłsudskiites' were the supporters of
     Marshal Józef Piłsudski (1867–1935) and his *Sanacja* regime in
     Poland, 1926–1939; the 'Sikorskiites' were followers of General
     Sikorski, a leading opponent of Piłsudski.
29. Ziarski-Kernberg, in Stachura (ed.), *Themes*, pp. 79–81.
30. The Thornton Private Papers, memorandum of 14 February 1949
     from the Catholic Council for Polish Welfare, intimating that at that
     time seven Polish priests were active in Scotland; see also Sword
     et al., *Formation*, pp. 430–41, and *'The Tablet'*, 7 May 1949. The
     wider picture is well covered in J. Gula, *The Roman Catholic Church
     in the History of the Polish Exiled Community in Britain, 1939–1950*
     (School of Slavonic and East European Studies, London, 1993).
31. J. Zubrzycki, *Polish Immigrants in Great Britain: A Study of
     Adjustment* (Nijhoff, The Hague, 1956), pp. 66, 81–6; E. Stadulis,
     'The Resettlement of Displaced Persons in the United Kingdom',
     Population Studies, 5 (1952), Part 3, pp. 207–37, esp. pp. 210, 219 ff.
     Some trade unions, such as the Transport and General Workers'
     Union and the General Municipal Workers' Union, were generally
     more welcoming. The numbers employed in civilian industry in 1946
     were two and a half million fewer than in 1939.
         The anguish caused to individuals by trade-union intransigence is
     poignantly illustrated by a letter of 19 March 1947 by Mrs Isa Serafin
     on behalf of her Polish husband to Mr John J. Campbell of the
     Scottish–Polish Society. The husband was offered a position as a cab-
     inetmaker by the Glasgow firm of A & W Robertson, only for the
     National Amalgamated Furnishing Trades' Association to block it by
     refusing Mr Serafin membership of the union (Thornton Private
     Papers, correspondence file of the Scottish–Polish Society).
32. Ziarski-Kernberg, in Stachura (ed.), *Themes*, p. 75; K. R. Sword,
     ' "Their Prospects will not be Bright": British Responses to the
     Problem of the Polish "Recalcitrants" ', *Journal of Contemporary
     History*, 21 (1986), pp. 367–90.
33. Sword *et al.*, *Formation*, pp. 265 ff.; Polish medical doctors fared
     better, thanks largely to the opportunities provided by the Polish
     School of Medicine in the University of Edinburgh, 1941–9. See
     W. Tomaszewski (ed.), *In the Dark Days of 1941: Fifty Years of the
     Polish School of Medicine, 1941–1991*. University of Edinburgh
     Jubilee Publication (privately published, Edinburgh, 1992).
34. *The Times* 21 May 1951.
35. Most revealing and informative on this subject is Keith Sword,
     Deportation and Exile: Poles in the Soviet Union, 1939–48
     (Macmillan, London, 1994), pp. 143–99.

36. Zubrzycki, *Polish Immigrants*, pp. 162ff.
37. For example, see the the strongly pro-Polish and anti-Communist reports, especially with regards the Warsaw Uprising, in the *Glasgow Observer and Scottish Catholic Herald* of 6 October 1944, and in similar vein in *The Tablet*, 7 May 1949.
38. The Thornton Private Papers, miscellaneous file, which includes sympathetic responses from a number of MPs.
39. Sword *et al.*, *Formation*, pp. 401, 404, n. 14.
40. A useful survey is L. Koczy, *The Scottish–Polish Society: Activities in the Second World War. An Historical Review* (Edinburgh, 1980).
41. The Thornton Private Papers, Membership Register of the Society's Glasgow branch, undated, but probably 1953.
42. *Ibid.*, correspondence file of the Scottish–Polish Society, 1943–4; *Glasgow Observer and Scottish Catholic Herald*, 6 October 1944. Among the MPs whom the Society contacted were Harold Macmillan, Rab Butler and Robert Boothby.
43. *Ibid.*, address by Campbell to the Society's AGM in Edinburgh on 30 July 1949, and letter of 27 January 1947 from Zygmunt Nagórski to Campbell concerning an anti-Polish item in a recent issue of the *Jewish Echo*.
44. *Ibid.*, correspondence of July 1949 between Campbell and Mr H. Przyborowski, head of the Agricultural School in Glasgow, concerning a controversial visit to the School by Teliga which ended in a fracas with some of the students. Also on file here is sharply worded correspondence about this matter between Przyborowski and Mr Frank H. Harrod, Secretary of the Committee for the Education of Poles in Great Britain, based in London.
45. Detailed coverage in J. T. Gross, *Polish Society under German Occupation: The Generalgouvernement, 1939–1944* (Princeton University Press, Princeton, NJ, 1979); R. C. Lukas, *The Forgotten Holocaust: The Poles under German Occupation, 1939–1944* (University Press of Kentucky, Lexington, 1986); G. C. Malcher, *Blank Pages: Soviet Genocide against the Polish People* (Pyrford Press, Woking, 1993).
46. *Census 1951 Scotland. Volume III, General Volume, op. cit.* Table 36, pp. 55 f.; and *ibid., Census 1981 Scotland. Summary. Volume I* (HMSO, Edinburgh, 1983), Table 51, pp. 55 ff., 62 ff.; K. Sword, *Identity in Flux: The Polish Community in Great Britain* (School of Slavonic and East European Studies, London, 1996), p. 77. For wider reference, B. Czaykowski and B. Sulik, *Polacy w Wielkiej Brytanii* (Paris, 1961), and Zubrzycki, *Polish Immigrants, op. cit.*
47. Estimate given by Consul General Paweł Dobrowolski in '*Gazeta. The Polish Scottish Gazette*', 1 (April–June 1995), p. 20.
48. From the author's private papers and testimomy from members of the Polish community.
49. Some background details in P. Wandycz, 'August Zalewski and His Times', *East European Quarterly*, 24 (1990), No. 4, pp. 409–23.

50. See discussion in Leslie (ed.), *History of Poland*, pp. 299–343.
51. A partial outline of the history of *Dom Sikorskiego* is provided by B. Wilson, *Dom Polski im. gen. Władysława Sikorskiego Towarzystwo Społeczno-Oświatowe w Glasgow* (Polish Educational and Social Association Ltd., Glasgow, 1989).
52. Private information to the author from various Polish sources.
53. See A. Zebrowska, *'Integration or Assimilation?' A Study of Second Generation Poles in England* (Ph.D., University of Surrey, 1986).
54. Sword, *Identity in Flux*, p. 136; and further information from officials of *The Polish Society*.
55. See below for more details.
56. See Giles Hart (ed.), *For Our Freedom and Yours: A History of the Polish Solidarity Campaign of Great Britain, 1980–1994* (London, 1995).
57. Reports in *The Glasgow Herald* and *The Scotsman*, June 1982. For background, see Gula, *The Roman Catholic Church in the History of the Polish Exiled Community in Great Britain*.
58. *The Times*, 23 December 1990.
59. J. Wasilewski, 'The Forming of the New Elite: How Much Nomenklatura is Left?' *Polish Sociological Review*, 110 (1995), No. 2, pp. 113–23.
60. The Polish Society: Minutes of Committee meetings, 1996–8.
61. Sword, *Identity in Flux*, p. 100.
62. *Gazeta* was launched as a quarterly newspaper in Spring 1995, but announced its closure in January 1998. Although it contained useful information about some Polish matters from time to time, it was generally of poor quality and expensive. Remarkably, the paper's demise thus coincided, more or less, with the ousting from office of the Communist-dominated government at the September 1997 parliamentary elections.
63. J. Zubrzycki, 'Whither Emigracja? The Future of the Polish Community in Great Britain', *The Polish Review*, 28 (1993), No. 4, pp. 391–406.

8 Polish Nationalism in the Post-Communist Era

In 1989/90, the Communist system of government in Poland formally came to an ignominious end. Stripped of the protective hand of the Soviet Union, which had been responsible for its establishment in 1944/45, the Communist regime was replaced by a parliamentary democracy, at the centre of which stood the most militant and successful patriotic movement in Poland since the end of the Second World War, *Solidarność* (Solidarity), under the charismatic leadership of Lech Wałęsa.[1] This putative metamorphosis in Poland's political situation represented the culmination of a deeply embedded disenchantment on the part of a substantial majority of the Polish people with a regime whose political, social and ethical values had always been alien to them. After all, during the inter-war period, the Communist Party of Poland (KPP) had attracted exiguous popular support, and was widely and rightly perceived to be a party whose ultimate objective was the destruction of the independent Polish state that had been created in 1918, and its subjugation to the Soviet Union. The remnants of this party, which Stalin himself had dissolved in 1938 because of its feeble performance and ideological unreliability, formed the basis of a revived wartime Communist movement sponsored by the Soviet dictator with the same aims as its pre-war predecessor.[2]

At Stalin's direction, and backed up by the Red Army and a massive security and police apparatus, the small band of Communists, subsequently styled the 'Polish United Workers' Party' (PZPR), emerged as the executor of Soviet will in post-war Poland. This imposed solution, which was accompanied by the brutal suppression of anti-Communist, nationalist forces in the late 1940s, effectively sealed Poland's fate as a repressed satellite in the Soviet empire for nearly half a century.[3] It was that legacy which *Solidarność* finally overthrew in a bloodless revolution, which

135

spearheaded a wider revolt against Communism throughout Eastern Europe.[4]

Solidarność, a movement which brought together in its ranks both the intelligentsia and workers on equal terms,[5] may be understood within the context of a popular Polish nationalism which, despite an extensive and penetrative programme of sovietization in the country as whole, had never been fundamentally absent from the political and social consciousness of the nation. In a very real sense, *Solidarność* was the heir of the intermittent but fruitless protests against the Communist system which had peppered Poland's post-war history. These manifestations of rejection, from the Poznań disturbances in 1956 to the workers' strikes and disorders of the 1970s, constituted the surest, most tangible indication of a significant divide between the ruling Communist élite and the mass of the population which *Solidarność* finally channelled into a more organized and coherent wave of patriotic revival.[6] In 1989/90, therefore, the *Solidarność* revolution intimated the legitimate recapture of Poland by the Poles and for the Poles.[7] If the rather muted sense of achievement among the Polish people contrasted sharply with the widespread euphoria experienced at the nation's rebirth in 1918 as an independent, sovereign state following a much longer period of foreign occupation and subordination, the mood of anticipation of better things to come was unmistakable. The view prevailed that at long last Poland would have the opportunity of picking up where she had been forced to leave off in 1939 or 1944, that is, to reconstruct the country along lines that were, however broadly defined, recognizably 'Polish'.

The certainties and optimism of that initial, transitional period, however, were largely dispelled by the political disappointments associated with what some observers had predicted as the inevitable disintegration of *Solidarność* into its constituent parts, and also, of equal importance, by the painful but necessary changes in the economy. The palpable anti-Communist consensus of 1989/90 gave way to internecine squabbling, factionalism and disillusionment, which allowed the former Communists, who had swiftly regrouped in the Social Democratic Party of Poland (SDRP), to exploit the situation to its own advantage: in alliance with the smaller Peasant Party, they secured victory in the 1993 elections.[8] *Solidarność* had always been a broad church which had been capable in the years of struggle against the Communist state of bringing together renegade Marxist intellectuals, including Adam Michnik, Jacek Kuron and Bronisław Geremek, as well as dissident nationalists, Catholics, social democrats and many others of varying and sometimes contradictory political opinion. But the demands and often sordid realities of power in national government forced underlying and dormant strains to the surface. Genuine differences over the degree of change necessary to arrest the decline of an economy based on the totalitarian, command model and the relative merits of a Western-style free market system, which Poland had been developing with increasing success before 1939, added to the rapidly emerging political and social confusion. Consensual politics, it soon became apparent, would form no part of the post-Communist process of adjustment. In other words, where once the all-embracing arms of a united *Solidarność* appeared likely to pave an uncontentious path of development for Poland, a situation fraught with progressively bitter recrimination and rivalry came into view.

In the political sphere, the *Solidarność* revolution proved to be a cautious affair, even after the first fully free parliamentary elections held in Poland for more than sixty years, in October 1991. The formation of a multitude of parties invited superficial but intrinsically valid parallels to be drawn with the earliest era of the Second Republic. No fewer than 29 parties were represented in the new *Sejm*. Cabinet instability soon became a striking feature of national politics, prompting the damning comment from overseas that Poland had 'a chaotic version of Italian proportional representation'.[9] Minor disagreements resulted in yet more splinter groups. The old political élite, the Communist *nomenklatura*, was not eliminated from positions of authority, continuing to wield significant influence, especially in the public sector, media, culture and the economy. It thus acted as an important brake on fully fledged democratic and parliamentary development. Political compromise of a most unsatisfactory kind was the outcome.[10]

This situation also hindered attempts to reconstruct the economy on a full capitalist basis. In the absence of a thoroughgoing political and governmental transformation, economic reform was, initially at least, doomed to degenerate into a series of half-measures. The patriotic spirit which had made possible the collapse of Communism in the first place proved unable, because of its political fragmentation, to carry the revolution to a natural conclusion; and so the revolution turned out to be something of a missed opportunity for sweeping political change. Even the Stalinist Constitution of 1952 remained in place, with a few relatively minor amendments, as a result of public apathy and resignation on the one hand, and of sectional infighting in parliament over a new version on the other.[11] One of the most complex questions to arise from this débâcle related to the future development of the concepts of patriotism and nationalism in Poland. Who or what would fill the vacuum created by the fall of *Solidarność* as a rallying-point for patriotic and nationalist aspiration?

Nationalism has been a crucial conditioning factor in the outlook and psyche of most Poles in modern times, from at least the Partitions of the late eighteenth century onwards. Where the Polish body politic ceased to have organized expression and thus became incapable of articulating traditional patriotic feeling,[12] the Catholic Church stepped forward to fill the gap. After all, for most Poles, Catholicism was and continues to be an integral part of their national identity. In the enforced absence of an independent Polish state from the 1790s until 1918, and particularly following the failed insurrection against the Russians in 1863–4, it fell to the Church to become the tangible embodiment of 'Polishness', which incorporated an unquenchable nationalism that had a cultural and literary as well as religious and spiritual content. This Polish nationalism was not a conceptually uniform phenomenon, but it nevertheless provided a focus for a politically dismembered nation and acted as the chief spur to efforts by the Poles to challenge their subservient status within the Russian, German and Habsburg empires of the nineteenth century. The Church remained standing, while these political episodes were ephemeral. Later, the drive for Polish independence that was led by two contrasting movements and personalities, the Polish Socialist Party of Józef Piłsudski and the National Democratic Party of Roman Dmowski, forced the Church over time to partially abandon its formerly neutral, party political role in favour of a close, sometimes active association with the National Democrats, whose nationalist, Catholic ethos was readily accepted.

During the Second Republic the Church consolidated its role as the ultimate non-political repository of a nationalism which was sharpened by the difficult problems confronting Poland at home and abroad.[13] Not only were Germany (particularly after 1933 under the National Socialists) and the Soviet Union under Stalin the avowed enemies of Poland, intent on reversing the terms of the Treaty of Versailles (notwithstanding Non-Aggression Pacts in 1934 and 1932 respectively), but a host of domestic economic, political and social matters also threatened her hard-won independence.[14] In particular the Polish state's uneasy relationship with its large ethnic minorities – Ukrainians, Germans, Byelorussians and Jews – especially during the disturbed years of the Depression, gave rise to a militant brand of nationalism which by the late 1930s was more or less shared by most sections of the previously hostile National Democratic and Piłsudski camps.[15] The Church, whose central place in society, and thus in the nationalist movement, had been institutionalized by the State–Vatican Concordat of 1925, demonstrated that authoritarian Catholicism blended effortlessly with nationalism. In this sense, therefore, the Church, which drew support from all sections of ethnic Polish society, including the peasantry, middle classes, landowners and, to a somewhat lesser degree, from the industrial proletariat and intelligentsia, not only legitimized herself but also personified mainstream Polish nationalism on the eve of the Second World War.[16]

The profound suffering and barbaric devastation endured by Poland during the war only served to strengthen further the role of the Church as the bedrock of nationalist sentiment in a situation where virtually all other institutional and organizational support systems dating from the pre-war period had disappeared.[17] The imposition of a Soviet-directed Communist dictatorship after 1945, in which the totalitarian imperative permitted no legal opposition, presented the Church with new challenges, not the least of which was that of sustaining traditional Polish nationalism alongside the internationalist credo of Marxism. The resulting necessary compromises under Cardinal Stefan Wyszyński[18] and, later, Cardinal Józef Glemp, did not always please nationalist Catholics, who thought the Church was at times too willing to seek accommodation with the regime. But, in extraordinarily difficult circumstances, where its very survival was never completely certain, the Church had to adopt policies and attitudes that were realistic, if far from ideal. It was essential that, at all costs, the Church retained a viable role as both the spiritual keeper and guardian of nationalist Poland.[19]

The finely tuned sense of realism which the Church developed under the Communists serves it well in the current situation where the new, democratic Poland needs to define the character of its nationalism within a Europe no longer divided by the Berlin Wall or overshadowed by the Soviet menace. There is a case for arguing, of course, that a Polish nationalism divested of its traditionally romantic dimension had already arisen from the sobering experience of the last war, particularly in relation to such cathartic episodes as the valiant but catastrophic Home Army Rising in Warsaw in 1944, and the arrant betrayal of Polish interests by the Western Powers at the conferences at Tehran (December 1943) and, above all, at Yalta (February 1945).[20] Through a long period of gestation in the post-war world, when the interests of the victorious allies of the war invariably took precedence over every other consideration, Polish nationalism was intrinsically different from earlier incarnations of the phenomenon in so far as Romantic-utopian ideals no longer exercised a decisive influence on either its substantive content or orientation.

A Church that, in the absence of any other national institution commanding widespread respect and affection, still remains the most potent symbol of Polish nationhood, is well placed to provide leadership to nationalist feeling in the aftermath of Communism. The encouragement and example given by the Polish Pope, John Paul II, are vital factors in this regard. The Catholic–Nationalist symbiosis may have undergone a degree of change since 1945, but it is still the most cherished and vibrant manifestation for Poles of their sense of national pride and identity.[21]

Post-Communist nationalism in Poland has inevitably assumed a certain party political expression. Although some observers have talked of a '*nomenklatura* nationalism' being promoted by former Communists,[22] the focus falls mainly on organizations and parties of the Right, including the Union for Realpolitik, Movement for the Republic (RdR), the Christian-National Union (ZChN) and Leszek Moczulski's better-known Confederation for an Independent Poland (KPN). The KPN, which originated in the 1970s when its small membership was constantly persecuted, espouses a radical form of nationalism which is in some ways reminiscent of that of the National Party (*Endecja*) and its offshoots in the late 1930s. The KPN is ultra-nationalist, vehemently anti-Communist, anti-Soviet (now Russian), and is also without doubt anti-Semitic.

A persistent critic of the Communist regime for its 'treasonable activities', the KPN has evolved also as one of the most vociferous opponents of the post-Communist order. As the foremost advocate of a policy of 'de-communisation', or 'lustration', whereby all traces, influence and power of the Communist past and its élite are to be erased from national life, including non-recognition of the validity of 'People's Poland', it has denounced the failure of government to carry this out as evidence that, first, *Solidarność*, and second, all successive governments from that led by Tadeusz Mazowiecki onwards, have been too weak and cowardly to merit the trust and allegiance of the Polish people. Compromise instead of decisive action in effecting a total political revolution, it asserts, has ensured that the sacrifices made by two generations of patriotic Poles since the war have been, in large measure, in vain.[23] Former President Wałęsa was as much a target for vilification from the KPN as the previous Red Establishment, and since the election to the Presidency in 1995 of Aleksander Kwaśniewski, a former Communist apparatchik, the attacks have reached an unprecedented level of stridency.

Although popular support for the KPN is exremelv limited in terms of membership and electoral backing – it barely cleared the 5 per cent threshold for representation in parliament at the 1993 elections – there is little doubt that it does articulate, albeit in a rather unrefined manner, some of the deeper anxieties felt by sections of the population, and not only among its disaffected younger elements. In so far as the designation 'middle-class' has meaning in an early post-Communist society, the KPN draws support from some of the Catholic middle-class intelligentsia in the professions, media and universities, though its principal source of support lies in the white-collar petty bourgeoisie and better-off peasantry. Disquiet over the consequences of rapid economic reform – price rises, higher rents, mass unemployment and influx of foreign capital – outrage at the continuing political and economic power of the old Communist *nomenklatura*, and the as yet unfulfilled promises to replace the Stalinist Constitution of 1952,[24] have naturally provided objective evidence for the KPN's allegation that nothing really fundamental of a political or constitutional nature has changed since the collapse of the old order. On the other hand, the KPN has little constructive comment to make about Poland's role in the new Europe, other than warning in vague language against the longer-term intentions of Russia and the Ukraine towards Poland, and of the dangers to Polish identity in an integrated Europe through membership of NATO and the European Union, as well as the consequences of foreign capital investment and property purchase.

The Christian political parties that have sprung up in the last few years, such as the Christian-National Union and the Catholic Action Group, compensate for organizational weakness by their wholehearted commitment to replacing Marxist influence in society at large with an unashamedly conservative Catholic moral and ethical code. They argue, and not without reason, that despite the natural antipathy of an overwhelming majority of Poles to Communism and Marxism, nearly half a century of these state-propagated dogmas have left a nefarious imprint on social and moral attitudes which must be eradicated at the earliest possible date. The Church has spoken repeatedly of a spiritual vacuum which can only be filled with Catholic principles and practice. Consequently, these parties enjoy the approval and often the active support of the Church, especially where vital issues such as abortion, divorce, religious instruction in schools and the Christian basis of a new constitution are concerned: there are clearly echoes here of the Church's support for the *Endecja* in the Second Republic.

The return to power of the former Communists in Autumn 1993 halted the Church's advance for the next four years, particularly as these matters were central to debate during the election of that year. Eventual success, however, in the present situation where the Centre-Right has returned to office following the September 1997 elections, would not only confirm the position of the Church and Catholicism generally, but would also consolidate Poland's status as the most fervently Catholic country in Europe – or, in short, would re-establish the status enjoyed by the Second Republic during the inter-war period. Simultaneously, such a reaffirmation of Catholic values and influence would denote a revitalization of Catholicism as an integral component of post-Communist Polish nationalism. This is not to deny, of course, that there are proponents of anti-clericalism and secularism; they are not confined by any means to the former Communist *milieu*, and the two European-style liberal parties, the Democratic Union and the Liberal Democratic Congress, would be included in them, but their appeals are predicated on the scale of economic misery rather than on an understanding of acute spiritual unease.

The increasingly apparent convergence of Catholicism and nationalism ineluctably leads to a consideration of the complex and extremely sensitive role of anti-Semitism in contemporary Poland, though the historical antecedents can hardly be ignored, especially in view of the pivotal experience of the Holocaust, the organized extermination of millions of Jews on Polish soil by Hitler's Third Reich.[25] Despite the enlightened policy of toleration adopted towards Jews by the medieval Polish kings, the relationship in more modern times between ethnic Poles and this important minority community has never been easy. Until the recreation of an independent Polish state in 1918, the anti-Semitism of Poles, which was notably strong in the countryside among the peasantry, was based largely on traditional Christian hostility to the alleged 'murderers of Christ', and on popular resentment at the considerable commercial and financial power of Jews. Amidst the profound economic and political instability that accompanied the launching of the new state, however, a definite political dimension to Polish anti-Semitism had been added from several sources. The chauvinistic National Democratic Party, one of the primary driving forces behind the attainment of independence and the single most important party in government until the Piłsudski coup of 1926, was overtly anti-Semitic. With its large popular following and advocacy of the concept of 'polonization', the party ensured that anti-Semitism was given a prominent place on the political agenda. This unfortunate development can also be explained to some extent in relation to the Jews themselves.

They constituted a substantial, visible community, particularly in major cities, such as Warsaw, Kraków, Łódź, Lwów and others, and were distinctive very often on account of their dress, religious practices, speech and customs. Their conspicuous presence in certain sectors of the economy and in a number of the liberal professions, including medicine, the law and journalism, further encouraged hostility from ethnic Poles in that strained period of history. Moreover, of vital significance for popular perceptions in the political arena was the widely held suspicion of Jewish disloyalty towards the Polish state. This distrust was a reaction to frequent denunciations of independent Poland by many Jewish leaders, such as Yitshak Gruenbaum; to the imposition on Poland in 1919 of a Minorities' Charter, mainly at the insistence of the American/British-led Jewish lobby at the Paris Peace Conference in 1919; to the support given by many Jews, especially in eastern Poland, to the invading Soviet Bolsheviks in 1920; and to the high profile of Jews in both the leadership and rank-and-file membership of the fledgling Communist Party of Poland, which was fiercely anti-Polish and, equally, pro-Soviet. At the very inception of the first independent Polish state for over 100 years, therefore, its existence was seen to have been put in jeopardy by a substantial number of its Jewish citizens. Although relations between ethnic Poles and Jews had their more auspicious moments, as when Marshal Piłsudski took control after 1926, the subsequent impact of the Depression, the concomitant ascent of Polish nationalism and the corresponding influence of Zionism on Jews produced further polarization and bitterness.[26]

The connection between this pre-war legacy and the Holocaust in the Second World War has been a matter of controversy for many years, though not necessarily in Poland during much of the Communist era.[27] Then, on Soviet instructions, questions of guilt, responsibility and historical antecedents were ignored by the

Polish regime for reasons of blatant political and ideological expediency. On certain occasions, most obviously in 1967/8, factions within the regime were not averse to whipping up a degree of popular anti-Semitism to help overcome a domestic crisis of one kind or another.[28] Since 1989/90, however, Polish nationalism has had no alternative but to come face to face for a second time this century with the issue, despite the fact that the once-numerous Jewish community has almost entirely vanished from Poland, which is more ethnically homogeneous than at any other time in her history. *Solidarność*, whose leadership included several Jewish intellectuals of Marxist provenance, disintegrated as a united entity before it could exert any real influence on this debate in the early 1990s, whereas the Church, if at first strangely ambivalent, has recently appeared increasingly conciliatory towards the Jewish interest.

The arena of discussion on the topic has been filled in large measure by the dictates of everyday political partisanship, as starkly exemplified, in the first instance, by the presidential campaign in December 1990, involving Wałęsa, Stanisław Tymiński and Tadeusz Mazowiecki, the object of anti-Semitic smears because of his Frankist background.[29] Although this politically motivated anti-Semitism did not at that point reach anything like the intensity it had provoked in the early 1920s and late 1930s, it was patently clear that a certain potential for anti-Semitism had survived the vicissitudes of the war and the post-war epoch. Extreme right-wing organizations, such as Bolesław Tejkowski's Polish National Party (PSN), openly distribute anti-Semitic literature, including the old canard, 'The Protocols of the Elders of Zion', and sponsor noisy street demonstrations with strong anti-Semitic overtones. The Israeli ambassador to Poland has been moved several times to make official protests directly to government and through the press. Following his election to the Presidency in 1990, Wałęsa, to his credit, publicly denounced anti-Semitism in all its forms of expression, and undertook a highly symbolic trip of reconciliation to Israel. At a special session of the *Knesset* on 20 May 1991 he poignantly begged Jews' forgiveness for the long history of Polish anti-Semitism.[30] He also lamented, more prosaically, the harm inflicted on the Polish economy as a result of anti-Semitic sentiments and activities, particularly regarding investment from the United States. None the less, the long dispute between the Church and Jewish representatives over the siting of a Carmelite convent at the former Auschwitz extermination camp was but one example of continuing tension in Polish–Jewish relations which is still keenly felt by broad segments of Polish society. For this reason, it might be argued that contemporary Polish nationalism is still firmly circumscribed by an outdated prejudice that is hindering its emergence into modernity.

Ghosts of the past continue to haunt Polish nationalist sentiment and to shape the country's understanding of its place in Europe in respect of its attitude to Germany and what is now Russia, Poland's traditional enemies to the West and East. Not only Poland's newly regained independence, but also the reunification of Germany and the collapse of the Soviet Union have conspired to create a situation radically different from the one which prevailed until the end of the last decade. With the artificial bonds of fraternal solidarity of the former Soviet satellite states irrevocably dissolved, and its entry to NATO blocked until 1997, Poland was compelled to review relationships in this sphere from a completely fresh perspective, while being ever-mindful of past burdens. Above all, these consisted of the Nazi–Soviet Pact of 1939, which had its genesis in the acerbic anti-Polish outlook of both Germany and Russia in the inter-war years; the primeval German and Soviet wartime occupations; the pusillanimous Katyń Massacre;[31] and, after 1945, Soviet domination. The Helsinki process, the framework provided by the Conference on Security and Co-operation, was a useful forum for broader discussion, but Poland's national interests and security remain intimately linked to the question of her western and eastern borders.

German reunification raised fears in Poland of the possibility of a revision of the Oder–Neisse Line, despite it having been confirmed as permanent in treaties with the Federal Republic in 1972 and the German Democratic Republic in 1950. The Bonn government had never been fully satisfied with the legality of these agreements, even during the period of Chancellor Willy Brandt's *Ostpolitik*. A later Chancellor, Helmut Kohl, at first appeared

reluctant, in early 1990, to give reunited Germany's final acceptance of the border with Poland. Strong anti-German feeling,
founded on pre-war and wartime memories, and kept alive by the
post-war Communist regime, reached dangerous heights of intensity as Polish nationalist demonstrations and official statements
became strident. In the event, the crisis was transient. Kohl bowed
to international pressure and agreed a binding settlement later that
same year which gave Poland security in terms of the territorial
status quo in the West.[32] This has not signalled, however, the
establishment of particularly friendly relations between the two
nations. Germans expelled from Poland after 1945 bitterly and
predictably attacked the settlement as 'a sell-out'. Anti-Polish feeling is widespread in Eastern Germany, and the rise of neo-Nazi
groups has provoked countless episodes of violence along the border. On the Polish side, this sort of behaviour merely reinforces
deeply entrenched suspicions of longer-term German intentions.

At the same time, the massive annexations of Poland's pre-war
Eastern provinces by the Soviet Union have not emerged as a
serious political issue between the two states at any time since
1945. During the Communist era the subject, like many others,
was simply taboo in Poland. But the post-Communist Polish
administrations have not felt inclined to demand revision either.
It seems that only a certain nebulous nostalgia for these once-so-
dear regions, including the historically Polish cities of Lwów
(now in the Ukraine) and Wilno (now in Lithuania), prevails
among Poles nowadays. However, there is no validity in international law for the Soviet aggrandizement, especially when it is
recalled that one and a half million Poles were forcibly deported
from the area by Stalin in 1939–41 and 1944–6.[33] It may not
be beyond the realm of possibility that a future, more stable and
self-assured Polish government, responding to nationalist demands,
will attempt to have matters finally regulated according to recognized legal principles; so that perhaps Lwów and Wilno might
not have been lost for ever. As it is, the centuries-old anti-Russian
component of Polish nationalism, which remained strong at
a popular as opposed to an official level under the Communists,
guarantees a continuation of underlying tension in the East,
despite the removal by 1992–4 of the huge contingent of Soviet

troops from Poland and tokens of friendship exchanged since then between the Polish, Russian and Ukrainian governments.

A new phase in Poland's retreat from the Communist era was signalled by the outcome of the parliamentary elections in September 1997, when the ruling Communist-dominated Democratic Left Alliance (SLD) was ousted from office by the Solidarity Election Action (AWS), a broad coalition of the reinvigorated union and three dozen right-wing and Catholic parties. This should mean at least the end of '*nomenklatura* nationalism', if it ever really existed other than in fanciful imaginations, and perhaps also the end of the Communists, 'former' or otherwise, as a power factor. On the other hand, it is too early to discern any substantive implications for mainstream nationalism. However, the somewhat muted papal visit to Poland in June 1997 and signs of a more widely disseminated secularism may be a reflection of a relative decline in the appeal and influence of the Church and, by association, in the Catholic ethos of Polish nationalism.[34]

There is obviously a series of unresolved domestic and external problems confronting the nationalist movement in Poland in the aftermath of the failure of Communism and its replacement by a parliamentary democratic system of government supported by a free-market capitalist economy. A modernized sense of national identity has yet to be forged from a combination of past virtues and present-day realities. The era of romantic nationalism in Poland is surely over. While every nation deserves to preserve and cherish what it considers to be worthwhile and inspiring from past historical experience – and Poland has never lacked myths and legends – it needs also to recognize that such ingredients have to be mixed with adjustments to changed circumstances. Polish nationalism, invariably caught down the ages between the competing cultures and aspirations of West and East, and suffering as a consequence, can strive to find a new and more satisfying niche within the framework of an enlarged European Union. The former President Wałęsa once lamented the length of time that has to elapse before Poland is likely to be admitted to full membership – not until well into the new millennium – but the period of waiting can be put to constructive use.[35]

If the precise form to be assumed by Polish nationalism in the post-Communist era is not yet entirely certain, and it is axiomatic that it has to divest itself of some unwholesome historical baggage, such as anti-Semitism, there is nevertheless every prospect that it can make a valuable contribution to the creation of a new and attractive European order. In this process of redefinition Polish nationalism, in its cultural and political manifestations, will finally terminate links with Romanticism and move closer to the orbit of pragmatic realism, but without sacrificing its intrinsic character based on Catholicism, a sophisticated cultural heritage and a deep affinity with Western civilization.[36] It may well be that what eventually does emerge is an updated version of National Democratic ideology,[37] probably the most dynamic influence on twentieth-century Polish history, which even the Communists at one time tried to appropriate for their own political advantage. In this way, the best elements of the nationalist credo of 1939 could be expected to blend successfully with the nationalist experience of the immediate past and present, thus allowing Poland to forge a fresh identity as an independent and sovereign state in the Europe of the new millennium.[38]

NOTES

1. A full scholarly account of the development of *Solidarność* has not yet been written, but useful introductions are T. Garton Ash, *The Polish Revolution: Solidarity* (Jonathan Cape, London, 1983: new Penguin edition, London, 1991), and N. Ascherson, *The Polish August: The Self-Limiting Revolution* (Penguin, London, 1981). See also L. Wałęsa, *A Path of Hope: An Autobiography* (Pan Books, London, 1988), esp. pp. 93–107, 115–35, 139–243.

2. Some details in M. K. Dziewanowski, *The Communist Party of Poland* (Harvard University Press, Cambridge, Mass., 1976), pp. 75–127, 139–54, and J. B. de Weydenthal, *The Communists of Poland: An Historical Outline* (Hoover Institution Press, Stanford, 1978), pp. 6–32; G. Simoncini, *The Communist Party of Poland, 1918–1929: A Study in Political Ideology* (Edwin Mellen Press, Lewiston, New York, 1993).

3. See the *Memorandum on the Liberation of Poland from Soviet Domination* (Polish Government-in-Exile, London, 1989).

4. Coverage in T. Garton Ash, *We the People: The Revolution of '89, witnessed in Warsaw, Budapest, Berlin and Prague* (Granta, London, 1990); I. Banac (ed.), *Eastern Europe in Revolution* (Cornell University Press, Ithaca, 1992); R. East, *Revolutions in Eastern Europe* (Pinter, London, 1992); M. Frankland, *The Patriot's Revolution: How Eastern Europe Won its Freedom* (London, 1990), esp. pp. 160–88; M. Glenny, *The Rebirth of History: Eastern Europe in the Age of Democracy* (Penguin, London, 1990); G. Stokes, *The Walls Came Tumbling Down* (Oxford University Press, 1993).

5. Two recent studies argue (unconvincingly) that *Solidarność* was primarily a workers' movement: L. Goodwyn, *Breaking the Barrier: The Rise of Solidarity in Poland* (New York, 1991), and R. Laba, *The Roots of Solidarity: A Political Sociology of Poland's Working-Class Democratization* (Princeton University Press, Princeton, New Jersey, 1991).

6. Detailed surveys in J. Karpiński, *Countdown: The Polish Upheavals of 1956, 1968, 1970, 1976, 1980...* (New York, 1982); P. Raina, *Political Opposition in Poland, 1954–1977* (London, 1978); and J. J. Lipski, *KOR: A History of the Workers' Defense Committee in Poland, 1976–1981* (University of California Press, Berkeley, 1985).

7. Z. Brzeziński, 'Post-Communist Nationalism', *Foreign Affairs*, 48 (1989/90, Winter), pp. 1–25.

8. *The Times*, 22 September 1993.

9. *Ibid.*, 6 May 1992, leader article.

10. J. Wasilewski, 'The Forming of the New Elite: How Much Nomenklatura is Left?' *Polish Sociological Review*, 110 (1995), No. 2, pp. 113–23; and A. Podgórecki, 'The Communist and Post-Communist Nomenklature', *ibid.*, 106 (1994). No. 2, pp. 111–23.

11. A. M. Cirtautas, 'Constitutional Development in Post-Communist Poland', *Polish Sociological Review*, 113 (1996), No. 1, pp. 17–24; and J. P. Holc, 'Liberalism and the Construction of the Democratic Subject in Postcommunism; the Case of Poland', *Slavic Review*, 56 (1997), No. 3, pp. 401–27.

12. Discussed in A. Walicki, *Philosophy and Romantic Nationalism: The Case of Poland* (Clarendon Press, Oxford, 1982), esp. Part 3; P. Brock, *Polish Nationalism* (New York, 1968). For a broader analysis, E. J. Hobsbawm, *Nations and Nationalism since 1780: Programme, Myth and Reality* (Cambridge University Press, 1991).

13. E. D. Wynot, 'The Catholic Church and the Polish State, 1935–1939', *Journal of Church and State*, 15 (1973), pp. 223–40.

14. A useful discussion of economic problems at the outset in P. Latawski (ed.), *The Reconstruction of Poland* (Macmillan, London, 1992).

15. E. D. Wynot, *Polish Politics in Transition: The Camp of National Unity and the Struggle for Power, 1935–1939* (University of Georgia Press, Athens, Georgia, 1974).

16. Wynot, 'The Catholic Church and the Polish State'.

17. Polish Ministry of Information, *The German New Order in Poland* (Hutchinson, London, 1942), pp. 317–402; more broadly, J. T. Gross,

Polish Society under German Occupation: The Generalgouvernement, 1939–1944 (Princeton University Press, Princeton, New Jersey, 1979); J. Garliński, *Poland in the Second World War* (Macmillan, London, 1985).

18. A. Micewski, *Cardinal Wyszyński. A Biography* (San Diego, 1984), pp. 88 ff., 110 ff.

19. A comparative perspective is outlined in P. Michel, *Politics and Religion in Eastern Europe: Catholicism in Hungary, Poland and Czechoslovakia* (Routledge, London, 1991); for Poland, pp. 62–70, 74–101, 108–16, 133–70.

20. See Polish Government-in-Exile, *The Yalta Agreements*, ed. Zygmunt C. Szkopiak (London, 1986); J. Karski, *The Great Powers and Poland, 1919–1945: From Versailles to Yalta* (University Press of America, New York, 1985); A. Polonsky (ed.), *The Great Powers and the Polish Question, 1941–1944* (Orbis, London, 1976).

21. B. Szajkowski, *Next to God: Poland: Politics and Religion in Contemporary Poland* (Pinter, London, 1983); J. Jerschina, 'The Catholic Church, the Communist State and the Polish People', in S. Gomułka and A. Polonsky (eds), *Polish Paradoxes* (Routledge, London, 1990), pp. 76–96.

22. Wojciech Roszkowski, 'Nationalism in East Central Europe: Old Wine in New Bottles?', in P. Latawski (ed.), *Contemporary Nationalism in East Central Europe* (Macmillan, London, 1995), pp. 13–24.

23. Information on the KPN from articles in *Gazeta Wyborcza*, 1989–96; see also M. Kula, *Narodowe i rewolucyjne* (Więź, Warsaw, 1991), pp. 30–83.

24. Cirtautas, 'Constitutional Development', *op. cit.*

25. From the large literature on the Jews: C. Abramsky, M. Jachimczyk and A. Polonsky (eds), *The Jews in Poland* (Basil Blackwell, Oxford, 1986); Y. Gutman, E. Mendelsohn, J. Reinharz and C. Shmeruk (eds), *The Jews of Poland Between Two World Wars* (University Press of New England, Hanover, 1989); J. Marcus, *Social and Political History of the Jews in Poland, 1919–1939* (Mouton, New York, 1983); N. Davies, *God's Playground: A History of Poland. Volume II, 1795 to the Present* (Clarendon Press, Oxford, 1981), pp. 254–66.

26. P. D. Stachura, 'The Polish–Jewish Symbiosis in the Second Republic, 1918–1939', earlier in this volume.

27. A. Polonsky (ed.), *'My Brother's Keeper?' Recent Polish Debates on the Holocaust* (Routledge, London, 1990), Introduction; D. Engel, *In the Shadow of Auschwitz: The Polish Government-in-Exile and the Jews, 1939–1942* (University of North Carolina Press, Chapel Hill, 1987), ch. 1.

28. M. Chęciński, *Poland: Communism, Nationalism, Anti-Semitism* (Karz Kohl, New York, 1982, pp. 156–73.

29. *The Times*, 15 November 1990; K. Gebert, 'Anti-Semitism in the 1990 Polish Presidential Election', *Social Research*, 57 (Winter 1991), pp. 723–55, 'Frankist' refers to a Jewish sect in the eighteenth century in Poland which converted to Catholicism.

30. *The Times*, 21 May and 5 November 1991.
31. The Soviet government finally admitted responsibility for the Katyń outrage on 13 April 1990, and in Autumn 1992 President Boris Yeltsin put the seal on this chapter when he handed over to the Polish authorities documents proving Stalin's authorization of the massacre. The truth had been established many years previously by Polish sources, for example, in J. K. Zawodny, *Death in the Forest: The Story of the Katyń Massacre* (Macmillan, London, 1971), and the Polish Cultural Foundation; *The Crime of Katyń: Facts and Documents* (Caldra House, London, 1965).
32 The background is sketched, perhaps too optimistically, by W. W. Kulski, *Germany and Poland: From War to Peaceful Relations* (Syracuse University Press, Syracuse, NY, 1976), ch. 3. See further M. Ludwig, 'The Foreign Policy of the New Polish Government and the German Question', *Politics and Society in Germany, Austria and Switzerland*, 3 (1991), No. 2, pp. 1–18, and G. Hendriks, 'The Oder–Neisse Line Revisited: German Unification and Poland's Western Border', *ibid.*, 4 (1992), No. 3, pp. 1–17.
33. K. Sword, *Deportation and Exile: Poles in the Soviet Union, 1939–48* (Macmillian, London, 1994), pp. 1–27, 143–73; J. T. Gross, *Revolution from Abroad: The Soviet Conquest of Poland's Western Ukraine and Western Byelorussia* (Princeton University Press, Princeton, 1988).
34. *The Times*, 3 June 1997.
35. *Ibid.*, 20 November 1992.
36. Frances Millard, 'Nationalism in Poland', in Latawski (ed.), *Contemporary Nationalism*, pp. 105–26.
37. As articulated above all by R. Dmowski. For example, *Myśli nowoczesnego Polaka* (Lwów, 1903), and *Separatyzm żydowski i jego źródła* (Warsaw, 1909).
38. For views on the notion of the 'New Europe', see B. Nelson, D. Roberts, W. Veit (eds), *The Idea of Europe: Problems of National and Transnational Identity* (Oxford University Press, 1992); G. Frost and A. McHallam (eds), *In Search of Stability: Europe's Unfinished Revolution* (Adamantine Press, London, 1992); J. Held (ed.), *Democracy and Right-Wing Politics in Eastern Europe in the 1990s* (Boulder, Colo., 1993).

Conclusion:
Poland – The Millennial
Perspective

For Poland, the twentieth century has twisted and turned to sculpt a series of distinctive epochs: the turbulent times from the turn of the century, through the First World War, until the attainment of freedom and independence in a re-established sovereign state; the at once exciting and depressing inter-war era, when successes in many important fields mingled with some unequivocal failures in others; the heroic experience of the Second World War, during which the Polish nation defied the best efforts of Nazi and Soviet invasion, partition and occupation to destroy it; the tragic early post-war years as the Soviet Union, with the complicity of Poland's erstwhile Allies, imposed Communism, followed by a sorrowful half a century or so of being caged behind the 'Iron Curtain' and reduced to the status of an abject Soviet satellite. Finally, the last decade of the century has happily witnessed the disintegration of Communism and its replacement, for the second time this century, by parliamentary democracy and capitalism – the hopeful and optimistic phase. Few European countries have experienced such vicissitudes, which have also included drastic changes to Poland's territorial shape and to the size, location and composition of its population. Having begun the century as a multicultural and multi-ethnic entity, it was transformed after 1945 into the most comprehensively homogeneous Polish state and society in history, albeit within an alien and generally detested ideological and political system.

Poland's development after 1900 has brought out the best and the worst elements in the country's character, the good and the bad, as it were, an antithesis that is probably most poignantly conveyed through the quality and stature of its most prominent leaders. On the one hand, there is the towering personality of Marshal Józef Piłsudski, still much revered in contemporary

Poland, accompanied by, among others, Poland's leading ideologue, Roman Dmowski, her cultural icon, Ignacy Paderewski, her military heroes General Władysław Sikorski, General Władysław Anders and General Stanisław Maczek and, more recently, the populist Lech Wałęsa, in his role as leader of *Solidarność*. On the other hand, this group of inspirational Poles stands in the starkest possible contrast to the discredited, rather pathetic figures of Bolesław Bierut, Władysław Gomułka, Edward Gierek, General Wojciech Jaruzelski and their ilk.

As the new millennium approaches, what can be said of Poland's prospects? How will it respond to the freshly beckoning challenges of the twenty-first century? The signs, to put it briefly, are somewhat mixed, even confusing. The 1990s, which were inaugurated with renewed hope and national pride in the shape of the Third Polish Republic, have resulted in a number of serious economic and social tribulations in response to the extremely rapid, brusque introduction of the free market and its associated materialist values. In turn, these have led to unexpected political consequences, most notably the return to government in 1993 of the 'reformed' Communists who, despite being ousted in 1997, continue to wield a significant degree of power in major institutions and spheres of national life, and the election in 1995 of a one-time Communist apparatchik to the Presidency.

Many sympathetic foreign observers of the Polish scene, in particular, have found these events rather shocking and incomprehensible. What was the struggle against Communism all about, after all, if, within a few years of it collapsing in total ignominy, its representatives, those who had accepted Poland's subservience to and exploitation by the Soviet Union over so many years, were once more installed in power, not by force or decree, but by democratic choice? Clearly, the Poles are often disconcertingly difficult to fathom. In any case, most would agree that the ineluctable imprint of Communism on them will take at least several generations to expunge. In the meantime, the Poles will be in a transitional stage, though still in a position to enjoy important advantages which were not available to them during the Second Republic, especially Poland's gradual reintegration into Western structures (NATO and subsequently, it is to be hoped, the European Union) and the absence of a threat to its independence from Germany and Russia, even if the latter, disorientated, backward and relatively weak, remains an imponderable quantity.

On balance, there are perhaps sufficient grounds to hope that, given the opportunity, time and encouragement, Poland, with its inherent, well-tested resilience and talent, can emulate the positive aspects of the inter-war Republic while avoiding its mistakes, thus allowing it, in partnership with friendly neighbours, to make a vibrant and worthwhile contribution to the evolution of Europe beyond the year 2000.

Appendix I

1903   Publication of Roman Dmowski's 'Myśli nowoczesnego Polaka' ('Thoughts of a Modern Pole')

1905–7   Revolution in Congress Kingdom

1906–7   School strikes in Prussian Poland

1906   Polish Socialist Party (PPS) splits (November)

1908   Union of Active Struggle (ZWC) set up in Lwów

1910   Riflemen's Association formed in Lwów

1912   National Democrats organise boycott of Jewish businesses in Warsaw

1914   Outbreak of the First World War; Proclamation (14 August) by the Russian Commander-in-Chief, the Grand Duke Nicholas, promising limited autonomy for the Poles under Tsarist tutelage; Formation of the Polish Legions by Józef Piłsudski

          The Polish National Committee established to promote the Polish cause with Russia

1915   German forces expel the Russians from Warsaw (August)

1916   By 'The Two Emperors' Manifesto', the Central Powers restore the Kingdom of Poland in close union with them (5 November)

1917   President Woodrow Wilson intimates to the American Senate his support for an independent Poland (January)

          Manifesto of the Provisional Government in Russia promising an independent Poland, linked militarily to Russia (March); France allows the creation of a Polish army on its soil (June)

          Piłsudski imprisoned by the Germans in Magdeburg for refusing to help set up a Polish army (*Polnische Wehrmacht*) to aid the Central Powers (July)

          The Polish National Committee re-established in Lausanne, then Paris (August)

          Regency Council created in Warsaw by the Central Powers (October)

1918   President Wilson's 14 Points (January) include a commitment to an independent Poland with access to the sea (Point 13)

          The Allies declare their support for an independent Poland (June)

          Beginning (1 November) of Polish-Ukrainian struggle for Lwów and Eastern Galicia; Provisional Government of 'Polish People's Republic' set up (7 November) in Lublin under Ignacy Daszyński; Piłsudski released from German captivity

          Piłsudski appointed (11 November) C-in-C of Polish forces and Provisional Head of State (14 November); Government formed under Jędrzej Moraczewski

Arrival of Ignacy Paderewski in Poznań leads to Polish rising (27 December)

1919   Beginning of Polish–Soviet War; Paderewski appointed Prime Minister; Elections for a Constituent *Sejm* (all in January)

Provisional (Small) Constitution passed (February)

Treaty of Versailles, signed for Poland by Paderewski and Dmowski (June)

Polish forces finally crush the Ukrainian nationalists to secure Eastern Galicia (July)

First Polish Rising in Upper Silesia (August)

1920   Piłsudski awarded title of 'First Marshal of Poland' (March, conferred in November)

Polish alliance (April) with the Ukrainians under Semen Petliura against Soviet Russia

Agrarian Reform Act (July)

Battle of Warsaw (August) ('Miracle on the Vistula'); momentous Polish victory over the Red Army; hereafter 'Polish Soldiers' Day', celebrated annually on 15 August

Second Polish Rising in Upper Silesia (August)

1921   Franco–Polish alliance (February); Polish–Romanian alliance (March)

New Constitution passed by *Sejm*; Treaty of Riga ends Polish–Soviet War; Plebiscite in Upper Silesia (all in March)

Third Polish Rising in Upper Silesia (May), led by Wojciech Korfanty

First National Census (September) records Polish population of 27.2 million

1922   Seym approves (September) building of new port of Gdynia (begun 1924)

Gabriel Narutowicz elected first President of Poland, but assassinated (December)

General Władysław Sikorski appointed Premier and Stanisław Wojciechowski elected the new President of Poland (December)

1923   Ambassadors' Conference recognises Poland's eastern border (March)

Piłsudski resigns his last official posts and goes into retirement (July)

1924   Bank of Poland created; the *złoty* is the new currency (April)

1925   Polish–Vatican Concordat (February); Polish–German Tariff War begins (to 1934)

Agreement (*Ugoda*) between Polish Government and Jewish Club in *Sejm* (July)

Second Agrarian Reform Act (December)

1926   *Coup d'état* by Marshal Piłsudski (May); Ignacy Mościcki elected President of Poland; formation of the right-wing Camp of Great Poland under Dmowski (December)

1927   'Stabilization Loan' of 62 million US dollars to Poland (October)

1928	Creation of Non-Party Bloc for Cooperation with the Government (BBWR) (January)
1929	Treasury Minister Gabriel Czechowicz resigns over financial scandal (March)
	Exhibition in Poznań (May) of Polish achievements since 1918
1930	The Depression begins
	'Pacification' of Eastern Galicia by Polish forces in response to Ukrainian terrorism
1931	A united Peasant Party (SL) formed (March)
	Second National Census records Polish population of 31.9 million (December)
1932	Polish–Soviet Non-Aggression Pact (July)
	Józef Beck replaces August Zalewski as Foreign Minister (November)
1933	Mościcki re-elected President of Poland (May)
1934	Polish–German Non-Aggression Pact (January)
1935	Introduction of new Constitution (April)
	Death of Marshal Piłsudski (12 May)
1936	Launch of government industrial strategy around the new Central Industrial Region
1937	Camp of National Unity (OZON) set up by government to rally all patriotic forces
1938	Poland recovers Cieszyn from Czechoslovakia (October)
1939	Death of Roman Dmowski (January); British guarantee to Poland (March)
	Nazi–Soviet Pact and Anglo–Polish Treaty (August); Germany invades Poland (1 September)
	Soviet Union invades Poland (17 September)
	General Sikorski heads Polish government-in-exile and Polish Armed Forces, based in Paris, then London (from June 1940)
1939–41	Nazi and Soviet reign of terror in Poland: mass killings and deportations
1941	Sikorski–Maisky Agreement (July) regulates Polish–Soviet relations
1942	Establishment of the Home Army (AK) as the main armed resistance in Poland
	Council for Aid to Jews set up in Warsaw by the Delegatura of the Polish government
1943	Stalin sets up the Communist 'Union of Polish Patriots' (March)
	The Katyń massacre uncovered (April)
	Jewish Ghetto Uprising in Warsaw (April–May)
	Death of General Sikorski (July)
	Allied Conference at Tehran (November–December)
1944	Soviet forces enter pre-war Polish territory (January)
	Victory for the Second Polish Corps at Monte Cassino (May)
	Stalin creates the Communist 'Polish Committee of National Liberation', which issues the 'Lublin Manifesto' (July)

	Warsaw Uprising by the Home Army (August–October)
	The First Polish Armoured Division plays a pivotal role in the Normandy Campaign
1945	Allied Conference at Yalta (February): Poland 'sold out' to the Soviets
	Formation of 'Provisional Government of National Unity' under Soviet control
	The Allies withdraw recognition from the Polish government in London in favour of the latter (July): Poland now 'People's Poland'
	Allied Conference at Potsdam (July–August)
1946	Kielce pogrom (42 Jews killed)
1947	Communist-controlled elections in Poland, thus violating the Yalta agreement
	Bolesław Bierut President of Poland (to 1952)
1948	Creation of United Polish Workers' Party (Communist) as ruling élite
1949	Bierut appointed Head of State and Polish Communist party chief (November)
1952	Soviet-styled Constitution introduced in Poland (22 July)
1953	Death of Stalin; Cardinal Stefan Wyszyński imprisoned (until 1956) by the regime
1955	Poland joins the Warsaw Pact
1956	Riots in Poznań against the regime; Władysław Gomułka appointed new Party chief
1968	Wave of Communist-inspired anti-Semitism leads to mass exodus of Jews from Poland
1970	Polish–West German treaty formally recognizes the Oder-Neisse border
	Anti-regime riots in Gdańsk claim over 300 lives (December); Gomułka resigns, and replaced by Edward Gierek
1976	Workers' Defence Committee (KOR) set up
1978	Karol Wojtyła, Archbishop of Kraków, elected Pope as John Paul II (16 October)
1979	First Papal visit to Poland
1980	Gierek replaced as Communist party head by Stanisław Kania (September)
	Birth of *Solidarność* (September), led by Lech Wałęsa
1981	Death of Cardinal Wyszyński; General Wojciech Jaruzelski new Party chief and proclaims martial law (December)
1983	Second Papal visit to Poland
1984	Polish security police murder Father Jerzy Popiełuszko, an outspoken anti-Communist
1987	Third Papal visit to Poland
1989	Round Table talks between regime and opposition; elections produce landslide victory for *Solidarność* (June); Tadeusz Mazowiecki appointed first non-Communist Premier of post-war Poland

1990	Wałęsa elected (December) President of Poland (now the Third Polish Republic)
	Polish Government-in-Exile in London formally disbands itself and returns seal of office to President Wałęsa
	Restoration of traditional patriotic symbols (crowned eagle) and celebrations (3 May, 15 August and 11 November)
1991	Fourth Papal visit to Poland; Polish economy rapidly decentralized and deregulated
1992	Withdrawal of Soviet troops from Poland, ending almost 50 years of occupation
1993	Parliamentary elections return 'reformed' Communists to power
1995	'Reformed' Communist Aleksander Kwaśniewski elected President of Poland after defeating Wałęsa
1997	Poland admitted to NATO
	Parliamentary elections sweep 'reformed' Communists from office (September), replaced by *Solidarność*-led Centre-Right alliance
1998	Poland takes first steps towards membership of the European Union (March)
	Bicentenary of birth of Adam Mickiewicz (1798–1855)
	Twentieth anniversary of the election of the 'Polish Pope'
1999	Presidential elections due (Autumn)

Appendix II

On 12 February at 7.30 pm, the British Foreign Office handed to the Polish Ambassador in London the text of the resolution concerning Poland adopted by President Roosevelt, Prime Minister Churchill and Marshal Stalin at the Yalta Conference between 4 and 11 February.

Before the Conference began, the Polish Government handed to the Governments of Great Britain and the United States a Memorandum in which the hope was expressed that these Governments would not be a party to any decisions regarding the allied Polish State without previous consultation and without the consent of the Polish Government. At the same time, the Polish Government declared itself willing to seek a solution of the dispute initiated by Soviet Russia through normal international procedure and with due respect for the rights of the parties concerned.

Despite this, the decisions of the Three Powers' Conference were prepared and taken not only without the participation and authorization of the Polish Government, but also without its knowledge. The method adopted in the case of Poland is a contradiction of the elementary principles binding the Allies, and constitutes a violation of the letter and spirit of the Atlantic Charter and the right of every nation to defend its own interest.

The Polish Government declares that the decision of the Three Powers' Conference concerning Poland cannot be recognized by the Polish Government and cannot bind the Polish nation.

The Polish Government will consider the severance of the Eastern half of the territory of Poland through the imposition of a Polish–Soviet frontier following along the so-called 'Curzon Line' as a fifth partition of Poland, now accomplished by her Allies.

The intention of the Three Powers to create a 'Provisional Polish Government of National Unity' by enlarging the foreign-appointed Lublin Committee with persons vaguely described as 'democratic leaders from Poland itself and Poles abroad' can only legalize Soviet interference in Polish internal affairs. As long as the territory of Poland remains under the sole occupation of Soviet troops, a Government of that kind will not safeguard to the Polish Nation, even in the presence of British and American diplomats, the unfettered right of free expression.

The Polish Government, who is the sole legal and generally recognized Government of Poland, and who for five and a half years directed the struggle of the Polish State and Nation against the Axis countries, both through the underground movement in the Homeland and through the Polish Armed Forces in all theatres of war, has expressed its readiness ... to co-operate in the creation of a Government in Poland that is truly representative of the will of the Polish nation. The Polish Government maintains this offer.

Source:
The Yalta Agreements. Documents prior to, during and after the Crimea Conference 1945. Published by the Polish Government-in- Exile, London, March 1986, and edited by Zygmunt C. Szkopiak, pp. 30–1 (with minor changes).

NOTES

The 'Polish Government' referred to in the text was set up in Autumn 1939 in France and continued to be recognized by the British and American governments (and others) until 5 July 1945, when that recognition was officially withdrawn.

The Polish Ambassador in London (line 2) from 1934 until 1945 was Count Edward Raczyński (1891–1992).

The Atlantic Charter (lines 14–15) of 14 August 1941 enunciated the basic principles by which the Allies were to conduct the war.

The 'Curzon Line' (line 20) was named after the British minister, Lord Curzon, who suggested it in 1920 as the frontier between Poland and Soviet Russia.

The 'Provisional Polish Government of National Unity' (lines 21–22) was created in 1945.

The 'Lublin Committee' (line 22) was composed of Polish Communists appointed by the Soviets.

The 'underground movement in the Homeland' (line 29) was the *Armia Krajowa* (Home Army), which was loyal to the Polish Government in London.

Appendix III

TELEGRAM SENT BY KING GEORGE VI TO THE PRESIDENT OF THE POLISH REPUBLIC ON THE OCCASION OF VE-DAY, LONDON, 6 MAY 1945

The President of the Polish Republic

It is with deep emotion, Mr President, that I send you this message of greeting on the day of final triumph over Germany.

It will be ever to Poland's honour that she resisted, alone, overwhelming forces of the German aggressor. For over five tragic years, the British and Polish nations have fought together against our brutal foe, years of terrible suffering for the people of Poland borne with a courage and endurance which has won my heartfelt admiration and sympathy.

The gallant Polish soldiers, sailors and airmen have fought beside my forces in many parts of the world, and everywhere have won their high regard. In particular, we in this country remember with gratitude the part played by Polish airmen in the Battle of Britain, which all the world recognises as a decisive moment in the war.

It is my earnest hope that Poland may, in the tasks of peace and international co-operation which now confront the Allied Nations, achieve the reward of all her courage and sacrifice.

Source:
The Yalta Agreements. Documents prior to, during and after the Crimea Conference 1945. Published by the Polish Government-in-Exile, London, March 1986, and edited by Zygmunt C. Szkopiak, p. 48.

NOTE

The President of the Polish Republic 1939–1947 was Władysław Raczkiewicz (1885–1947).

Select Bibliography

This list is restricted to books published in English.

GENERAL

Bromke, A., *The Meaning and Uses of Polish History* (Boulder, Colo., 1987)
Davies, N., *God's Playground: A History of Poland. Volume II: 1795 to the Present* (Oxford, 1981)
Davies, N., *Heart of Europe: A Short History of Poland* (Oxford, 1984)
Davies, N., *Sobieski's Legacy: Polish History, 1683–1983* (London, 1985)
Dziewanowski, M. K., *Poland in the Twentieth Century* (New York, 1977)
Halecki, O., *History of Poland* (London, 1977)
Landau, Z. and Tomaszewski, J., *The Polish Economy in the Twentieth Century* (London, 1985)
Leslie, R. F. (ed.), *The History of Poland since 1863* (London, 1983)
Reddaway, W. F. *et al.* (eds), *The Cambridge History of Poland. Volume 2: From Augustus II to Pilsudski (1697–1935)* (Cambridge, 1951)
Roos, H., *A History of Modern Poland* (London, 1966)
Stachura, P. D. (ed.), *Themes of Modern Polish History* (Glasgow, 1992)
Topolski, J., *An Outline History of Poland* (Warsaw, 1986)
Tymowski, M., *History of Poland* (Paris, 1986)
Zamoyski, A., *The Polish Way: A Thousand-Year History of the Poles and their Culture* (London, 1987)

THE PARTITIONIST ERA

Bartoszewski, W. and Polonsky, A. (eds), *The Jews in Warsaw: A History* (Oxford, 1991)
Blanke, R., *Prussian Poland in the German Empire, 1871–1900* (Boulder, Colo., 1981)
Blejwas, S. B., *Realism in Polish Politics: Warsaw Positivism and National Survival in Nineteenth-Century Poland* (New Haven, Conn., 1984)
Blit, L., *The Origins of Polish Socialism: The History and Ideas of the First Polish Socialist Party, 1878–1886* (London, 1971)
Blobaum, R. E., *Feliks Dzierżyński and the SDKPiL: A Study of the Origins of Polish Communism* (Boulder, Colo., 1984)
Blobaum, R. E., *Rewolucja: Russian Poland, 1904–1907* (Ithaca, New York, 1995)
Brock, P., *Nationalism and Populism in Partitioned Poland: Selected Essays* (London, 1968)

Bromke, A., *Poland's Politics: Idealism versus Realism* (Cambridge, Mass., 1967)

Chmielewski, E., *The Polish Question in the Russian State Duma* (Knoxsville, 1970)

Corrsin, S. D., *Warsaw Before the First World War: Poles and Jews in the Third City of the Russian Empire, 1880–1914* (Boulder, Colo., 1989)

Fountain, A. M., *Roman Dmowski: Party, Tactics, Ideology 1895–1907* (Boulder, Colo., 1980)

Hagen, W. W., *Germans, Poles and Jews: The Nationality Conflict in the Prussian East, 1772–1914* (Chicago, 1980)

Kieniewicz, S., *The Emancipation of the Polish Peasantry* (Chicago, 1969)

Naimark, N. M., *A History of the 'Proletariat': The Emergence of Marxism in the Kingdom of Poland, 1870–1887* (New York, 1979)

Narkiewicz, O. A., *The Green Flag: Polish Populist Politics, 1867–1970* (London, 1976)

Opalski, M. and Bartal, I., *Poles and Jews: A Failed Brotherhood* (Hanover, New England, 1993)

Trzeciakowski, L., *The Kulturkampf in Prussian Poland* (Boulder, Colo., 1990)

Walicki, A., *Philosophy and Romantic Nationalism: The Case of Poland* (Oxford, 1982)

Wandycz, P. S., *The Lands of Partitioned Poland, 1795–1918* (Seattle, 1974)

Woolf, L., *The Vatican and Poland in the Age of the Partitions* (Boulder, Colo., 1988)

THE FIRST WORLD WAR

Fischer, F., *Germany's Aims in the First World War* (New York, 1967)

Gerson, L. L., *Woodrow Wilson and the Rebirth of Poland, 1914–1920* (Hamden, Conn., 1972)

Komarnicki, T., *The Rebirth of the Polish Republic: A Study in the Diplomatic History of Europe, 1914–1920* (London, 1957)

Latawski, P. (ed.), *The Reconstruction of Poland, 1914–1923* (London, 1992)

Levene, M., *War, Jews and the New Europe: The Diplomacy of Lucien Wolf, 1914–1919* (Oxford, 1992)

Lundgreen-Nielsen, K., *The Polish Problem at the Paris Peace Conference: A Study of the Policies of the Great Powers and the Poles, 1918–1919* (Odense, 1979)

THE SECOND REPUBLIC, 1918–39

Abramsky, C., Jachimczyk, M., Polonsky, A. (eds), *The Jews in Poland* (Oxford, 1986)

Blanke, R., *Orphans of Versailles: The Germans in Western Poland, 1918–1939* (Lexington, 1993)

Carpenter, B., *The Poetic Avant-Garde in Poland, 1918–1939* (Seattle, 1983)

Cienciala, A. M., *Poland and the Western Powers, 1938–1939* (Toronto, 1968)

Cienciala, A. M. and Komarnicki, T., *From Versailles to Locarno. Keys to Polish Foreign Policy, 1919–1925* (Lawrence, Kansas, 1984)

Davies, N., *White Eagle, Red Star: The Polish–Soviet War, 1919–20* (London, 1972)

Dawidowicz, L., *The War Against the Jews, 1933–45* (London, 1975)

Debicki, R., *The Foreign Policy of Poland, 1919–1939* (New York, 1962)

Dziewanowski, M. K., *Joseph Pilsudski: A European Federalist, 1918–1922* (Stanford, Calif., 1969)

Dziewanowski, M. K., *The Communist Party of Poland: An Outline History* (Cambridge, Mass., 1976)

Garlicki, A., *Josef Pilsudski, 1867–1935* (New York, 1995)

Gromada, T. V. (ed.), *Essays on Poland's Foreign Policy, 1918–1939* (New York, 1970)

Gutman, Y. *et al.* (eds), *The Jews of Poland Between Two World Wars* (Hanover, New England, 1989)

Heller, C. S., *On the Edge of Destruction: Jews of Poland Between the Two World Wars* (New York, 1977)

Horak, S., *Poland and her National Minorities, 1919–39* (New York, 1961)

Jędrzejewicz, W., *Pilsudski: A Life for Poland* (New York, 1982)

Kapiszewski, A. (ed.), *Hugh Gibson and a Controversy over Polish-Jewish Relations after World War I: A Documentary History* (Kraków, 1991)

Karski, J., *The Great Powers and Poland, 1919–1945: From Versailles to Yalta* (New York, 1985)

Klimaszewski, B. (ed.), *An Outline History of Polish Culture* (Warsaw, 1978)

Korbel, J., *Poland Between East and West: Soviet and German Diplomacy Towards Poland, 1919–1933* (Princeton, 1963)

Korczyński, A. and Świętochowski, S. (eds), *Poland between Germany and Russia, 1926–1939* (New York, 1975)

Lewin, I. and Gelber, N. M., *A History of Polish Jewry during the Renewal of Poland* (New York, 1990)

Marcus, J., *Social and Political History of the Jews in Poland, 1919–1939* (New York, 1983)

Mendelsohn, E., *Zionism in Poland: The Formative Years, 1915–1926* (New Haven, 1981)

Mendelsohn, E., *On Modern Jewish Politics: The Interwar Years in Poland and America* (Oxford, 1993)

Miłosz, C., *The History of Polish Literature* (London, 1969)

Modras, R., *The Catholic Church and Antisemitism: Poland, 1933–1939* (New York, 1994)

Newman, S., *March 1939: The British Guarantee to Poland* (Oxford, 1976)

Palij, M., *The Ukrainian–Polish Defensive Alliance, 1919–1921* (Toronto, 1995)

Pease, N., *Poland, the United States, and the Stabilization of Europe, 1919–1933* (New York, 1986)

Polonsky, A., *Politics in Independent Poland: The Crisis of Constitutional Government* (Oxford, 1972)

Prażmowska, A., *Britain, Poland and the Eastern Front, 1939* (Cambridge, 1987)

Riekhoff, H. von, *German–Polish Relations, 1918–1933* (Baltimore, 1971)

Roszkowski, W., *Landowners in Poland, 1918–1939* (Cambridge, 1991)

Rothschild, J., *Piłsudski's Coup d'Etat* (New York, 1966)

Schatz, J., *The Generation: The Rise and Fall of the Jewish Communists of Poland* (Berkeley, 1991)

Simoncini, G., *The Communist Party of Poland, 1918–1929: A Study in Political Ideology* (New York, 1993)

Stachura, P. D. (ed.), *Poland Between the Wars, 1918–1939* (London, 1998)

Taylor, J. J., *The Economic Development of Poland, 1919–1950* (New York, 1952)

Wandycz, P. S., *France and her Eastern Allies, 1919–1925* (Minneapolis, 1962)

Wandycz, P. S., *Soviet–Polish Relations, 1917–1921* (Cambridge, Mass., 1969)

Wandycz, P. S., *The United States and Poland* (Cambridge, Mass., 1980)

Wandycz, P. S., *Polish Diplomacy 1914–1945: Aims and Achievements* (London, 1988)

Wandycz, P. S., *The Twilight of French Eastern Alliances, 1926–1936* (Princeton, 1988)

Watt, R. M., *Bitter Glory. Poland and Its Fate: 1918 to 1939* (New York, 1979)

Weinbaum, L., *A Marriage of Convenience: The New Zionist Organisation and the Polish Government, 1936–1939* (New York, 1993)

Weydenthal, J. B. de, *The Communists of Poland: An Historical Outline* (Stanford, 1978)

Wiles, T. (ed.), *Poland Between the Wars, 1918–1939* (Bloomington, 1989)

Wynot, E. D., *Polish Politics in Transition: The Camp of National Unity and the Struggle for Power, 1935–1939* (Athens, Georgia, 1974)

Wynot, E. D., *Warsaw Between the World Wars: Profile of the Capital City in a Developing Land, 1918–1939* (Boulder, Colo., 1983)

Zamoyski, A., *The Battle for the Marchlands* (Boulder, Colo., 1981)

Zweig, F., *Poland Between the Wars: A Critical Study of Social and Economic Change* (London, 1944)

Żółtowski, A., *Border of Europe: A Study of the Polish Eastern Provinces* (London, 1950)

POLAND IN THE SECOND WORLD WAR

Bartoszewski, W., *Warsaw Death Ring, 1939–1944* (Warsaw, 1968)

Bethell, N., *The War That Hitler Won* (London, 1972)

Ciechanowski, J. M., *The Warsaw Rising of 1944* (London, 1974)

Coutouvidis, J. and Reynolds, J. (eds), *Poland, 1939–1947* (Leicester, 1986)

Davies, N. and Polonsky, A. (eds), *Jews in Eastern Poland and the USSR, 1939–46* (London, 1991)

Dobroszycki, L., *Reptile Journalism: The Official Polish-Language Press under the Nazis* (New Haven, 1994)

Engel, D., *In the Shadow of Auschwitz: The Polish Government-in-Exile and the Jews, 1939–1942* (Chapel Hill, 1987)

Engel, D., *Facing a Holocaust: The Polish Government-in-Exile and the Jews, 1942–1945* (Chapel Hill, 1993)

Garliński, J., *Poland in the Second World War* (London, 1985)

Gross, J. T., *Polish Society under German Occupation: The General-gouvernement, 1939–1944* (Princeton, 1979)

Gross, J. T., *Revolution from Abroad: The Soviet Conquest of Poland's Western Ukraine and Western Byelorussia* (Princeton, 1988)

Gutman, Y., *The Jews of Warsaw, 1939–1943: Ghetto, Underground, Revolt* (Bloomington, 1982)

Hanson, J. K. M., *The Civilian Population and the Warsaw Uprising of 1944* (London, 1982)

Kacewicz, G. V., *Great Britain, the Soviet Union, and the Polish Government-in-Exile (1939–1945)* (The Hague, 1979)

Korboński, S., *The Polish Underground State: A Guide to the Underground, 1939–1945* (Boulder, Colo., 1978)

Korboński, S., *The Jews and Poles in World War II* (New York, 1989)

Lukas, R. C., *The Strange Allies: The United States and Poland, 1941–45* (Knoxsville, 1978)

Lukas, R. C., *The Forgotten Holocaust: The Poles under German Occupation, 1939–1944* (Lexington, 1986)

Malcher, G. C., *Blank Pages: Soviet Genocide against the Polish People* (Woking, 1993)

Pinchuk, B. C., *Shtetl Jews under Soviet Rule: Eastern Poland on the Eve of the Holocaust* (Oxford, 1990)

Polonsky, A. (ed.), *The Great Powers and the Polish Question, 1941–1945* (London, 1976)

Polonsky, A. (ed.), *'My Brother's Keeper.' Recent Polish Debates on the Holocaust* (London, 1990)

Prażmowska, A. J., *Britain and Poland, 1939–1943* (Cambridge, 1995)

Ringelbaum, E., *Polish–Jewish Relations during the Second World War* (Evanson, Ill., 1992)

Steinlauf, M. C., *Bondage to the Dead: Poland and the Memory of the Holocaust* (Syracuse, 1996)

Sword, K. (ed.), *Sikorski: Soldier and Statesman* (London, 1990)

Sword, K. (ed.), *The Soviet Takeover of the Polish Eastern Provinces, 1939–41* (London, 1991)

Sword, K., *Deportation and Exile: Poles in the Soviet Union, 1939–48* (London, 1994)

Sword, K., Davies, N., and Ciechanowski, J., *The Formation of the Polish Community in Great Britain, 1939–1950* (London, 1989)

Tec, N., *Christian Rescue of Jews in Nazi-Occupied Poland* (Oxford, 1985)

Terry, S. M., *Poland's Place in Europe: General Sikorski and the Origin of the Oder–Neisse Line, 1939–1943* (Princeton, 1983)

Zawodny, J. K., *Death in the Forest: The Story of the Katyń Massacre* (London, 1971)

Zawodny, J. K., *Nothing but Honour: The Story of the Warsaw Uprising* (London, 1978)

Zochowski, S., *British Policy in Relation to Poland in the Second World War* (New York, 1988)

Zubrzycki, J., *Polish Immigrants in Great Britain: A Study of Adjustment* (The Hague, 1956)

THE POST-WAR ERA

Andrews, N. G., *Poland, 1980–81: Solidarity versus the Party* (Washington, DC, 1985)

Ascherson, N., *The Polish August: The Self-Limiting Revolution* (London, 1981)

Bethell, N., *Gomułka, His Poland, His Communism* (New York, 1969)

Bromke, A. and Strong, J. W. (eds), *Gierek's Poland* (New York, 1973)

Brzeziński, M., *The Struggle for Constitutionalism in Poland* (London, 1997)

Chęciński, M., *Poland: Communism, Nationalism, Anti-Semitism* (New York, 1982)

Clarke, R. A. (ed.), *Poland: The Economy in the 1980s* (London, 1989)

Garton Ash, T., *The Polish Revolution: Solidarity* (London, 1983)

Goodwyn, L., *Breaking the Barriers: The Rise of Solidarity in Poland* (New York, 1991)

Gomulka, S. and Polonsky, A., *Polish Paradoxes* (London, 1990)

Hall, A., *The History and Development of the Political Parties in Poland* (London, 1991)

Kamiński, B., *The Collapse of State Socialism: the case of Poland* (Princeton, 1991)

Karpiński, J., *Countdown: The Polish Upheavals of 1956, 1968, 1970, 1976, 1980 ...* (New York, 1982)

Kaufman, M. T., *Mad Dreams, Saving Graces: Poland, a Nation in Conspiracy* (New York, 1989)

Kemp-Welsh, A. (ed.), *The Birth of Solidarity* (London, 1991)

Kersten, K., *The Establishment of Communist Rule in Poland, 1943–1948* (London, 1993)

Lepak, K. J., *Prelude to Solidarity: Poland and the Politics of the Gierek Regime* (New York, 1988)

Lipski, J. J., *KOR: A History of the Workers' Defense Committee in Poland, 1976–1981* (Berkeley, 1985)

Micewski, A., *Cardinal Wyszyński: A Biography* (San Diego, 1984)

Mikołajczyk, S., *The Rape of Poland: Pattern of Soviet Aggression* (New York, 1948)

Ost, D., *Solidarity and the Politics of Anti-Politics: Opposition and Reform in Poland since 1968* (Philadelphia, 1990)

Polonsky, A. and Drukier, B. (eds), *The Beginnings of Communist Rule in Poland, December 1943–June 1945* (London, 1980)

Prizel, I., Nitze, P. H., Michta, A. A. (eds), *Polish Foreign Policy Reconsidered: Challenges of Independence* (London, 1995)

Rachwald, A. R., *In Search of Poland: The Superpowers' Response to Solidarity, 1980–1989* (Stanford, Cal., 1990)

Raina, P., *Political Opposition in Poland, 1954–1977* (London, 1978)

Sandford, G., *Polish Communism in Crisis* (London, 1983)

Staniszkis, J., *Poland's Self-Limiting Revolution* (Princeton, 1984)

Starr, R. F., *Poland, 1944–1962: The Sovietization of a Captive People* (New Orleans, 1962)

Stehle, H., *The Independent Satellite: Society and Politics in Poland since 1945* (New York, 1965)

Szajkowski, B., *Next to God: Poland. Politics and Religion in Contemporary Poland* (London, 1983)

Taras, R., *Ideology in a Socialist State: Poland, 1956–1983* (Cambridge, 1984)

Tischner, J., *The Spirit of Solidarity* (San Francisco, 1984)

Torańska, T., *'Them': Stalin's Polish Puppets* (New York, 1987)

Torraine, A., Dubet, F., Wieviorka, M., Strzelecki, J., *Solidarity: Poland, 1980–81* (Cambridge, 1983)

Wałęsa, L., *A Path of Hope: An Autobiography* (London, 1987)

Weschler, L., *The Passion of Poland: From Solidarity through to the State of War* (New York, 1984)

Index